Making furniture for the Home

By the same author:
Projects and Designs in Woodwork (Batsford, 1981)
Projects and Designs in Metalwork (Batsford, 1981)

Making furniture for the Home

Ian Punter

St. Martin's Press
New York

MAKING FURNITURE FOR THE HOME.
Copyright © 1984 by Ian Punter. All rights reserved.
Printed in the United Kingdom. No part of this book
may be used or reproduced in any manner whatsoever
without written permission except in the case of brief
quotations embodied in critical articles or reviews. For
information, address St. Martin's Press, 175 Fifth
Avenue, New York, N.Y. 10010.

Library of Congress Catalogue Card Number 85–50142
ISBN 0-312-50122-6
First U.S. Edition
10 9 8 7 6 5 4 3 2 1

Contents

Foreword

There are many advantages and much satisfaction to be derived from the successful construction of items of furniture for the home. In some cases there may be a considerable financial saving to be made, or a better quality to be gained for the same cost as that of the bought article, but perhaps of greater significance is the fact that a piece of furniture can be made to satisfy fully the requirements of an individual situation. In this way the size, material and appearance of an item of furniture are within the control of the maker. This is not to say that there is not some well-designed and well-made furniture on the market at a reasonable price, and so there might be little point in attempting to make certain items.

Much thought has been given to the balance of the material in this book and a substantial technical section has been included for reference. It is intended that this will be used in conjunction with the suggestions in the project section, and it is hoped that readers will be encouraged not only to take up some of the project suggestions but also to initiate their own work, using the technical section for reference where necessary. Indeed, the projects themselves are not considered to be the answers to everyone's needs and it is expected that they will be adapted to suit individual requirements. The section dealing with plans has been included to help with the adaptation and preparation of designs, and it contains guidance for establishing seating positions, table heights, etc.

At the end of the book there is an extensive, illustrated woodworking glossary which will help in the identification of tools, materials and techniques and their correct usage. Portable power tools are mentioned in this section and throughout the book, but no attempt is made to instruct in the use of woodwork machinery and power tools. It is assumed that the owners of such machinery will follow the instructions which are relevant to the safe operation of a particular machine and will know the scale and type of work which the machine is able to tackle.   I.P.

Acknowledgements

The author is indebted to many manufacturers and suppliers for their willingness to provide information on their products. In particular the author wishes to thank those who were kind enough to supply photographs for this book, including Bahco Record Tools, Black & Decker, Neill Tools, Rabone Chesterman, Stanley Tools and Woodfit.

Measurements

Most of the metric measurements in the illustrations have been converted to the nearest $\frac{1}{8}$in where the measurements come to under 1in; over that to the nearest $\frac{1}{4}$in. (For greater accuracy consult the table on p.140).

Technical Section

1 Market forms of timber and manufactured board materials

HARDWOODS

Hardwoods are mostly available in boards of random width which are machine-planed to standard thicknesses. Typical thicknesses are 9, 12, 15 and 21mm ($\frac{3}{8}$, $\frac{1}{2}$, $\frac{5}{8}$ and $\frac{7}{8}$in) and the timber is costed at so much per square metre or yard.

Hardwoods are also available in fully prepared sections and some common examples are 21 × 21mm, 34 × 21mm, 34 × 34mm, 46 × 21mm and 46 × 46mm ($\frac{7}{8} \times \frac{7}{8}$in, $1\frac{1}{4} \times \frac{7}{8}$in, $1\frac{1}{4} \times 1\frac{1}{4}$in, $1\frac{3}{4} \times \frac{7}{8}$in and $1\frac{3}{4} \times 1\frac{3}{4}$in). These sections are costed at so much per linear metre or metre run (linear yard or yard run).

SOFTWOODS

Softwoods are normally supplied in boards of standard widths and thicknesses and can therefore be costed at so much per linear metre or metre run. The timber can be bought as *sawn* or *planed*, there being a slight cost advantage in buying sawn timber. When buying planed timber it is important to realise that it is produced by machine planing a standard sawn size and therefore will be 3 or 4mm (about $\frac{1}{8}$in) smaller.

Standard *sawn* sizes
Board thicknesses of 12, 16, 19, 22 and 25mm ($\frac{1}{2}$, $\frac{5}{8}$, $\frac{3}{4}$, $\frac{7}{8}$ and 1in).
Board widths of 150, 175, 200 and 225mm (6, 7, 8 and 9in).

Standard *planed* sizes
Board thicknesses of 9, 12, 15, 19 and 21mm ($\frac{3}{8}$, $\frac{1}{2}$, $\frac{5}{8}$, $\frac{3}{4}$ and $\frac{7}{8}$in).
Board widths of 150, 175, 200 and 225mm (6, 7, 8 and 9in).

Softwoods are also available in sections and a typical range of small sawn sections might be: 25 × 25mm, 38 × 25mm, 38 × 38mm, 50 × 25mm and 50 × 50mm (1 × 1in, $1\frac{1}{2}$ × 1in, $1\frac{1}{2}$ × $1\frac{1}{2}$in, 2 × 1in and 2 × 2in). If these sections were required machine-planed they would be: 21 × 21mm, 34 × 21mm, 34 × 34mm, 46 × 21mm and 45 × 45mm ($\frac{7}{8} \times \frac{7}{8}$in, $1\frac{1}{4} \times \frac{7}{8}$in, $1\frac{1}{4} \times 1\frac{1}{4}$in, $1\frac{3}{4} \times \frac{7}{8}$in and $1\frac{1}{4} \times 1\frac{1}{4}$in).

Larger softwood sawn sections may sometimes be required purely for their size or as a more economical means of producing smaller sections. Some examples of common sizes are: 38 × 150mm, 38 × 225mm, 50 × 150mm, 50 × 200mm, 63 × 200mm, 75 × 200mm and 75 × 225mm ($1\frac{1}{2}$ × 6in, $1\frac{1}{2}$ × $8\frac{3}{4}$in, 2 × 6in, 2 × 8in, $2\frac{1}{2}$ × 8in, 3 × 8in and 3 × $8\frac{3}{4}$in).

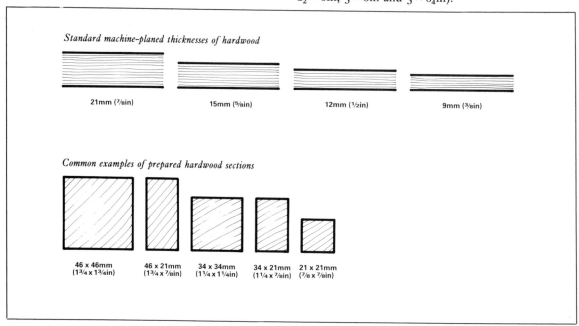

Standard machine-planed thicknesses of hardwood

21mm (7/8in)   15mm (5/8in)   12mm (1/2in)   9mm (3/8in)

Common examples of prepared hardwood sections

46 x 46mm (1¾ x 1¾in)   46 x 21mm (1¾ x 7/8in)   34 x 34mm (1¼ x 1¼in)   34 x 21mm (1¼ x 7/8in)   21 x 21mm (7/8 x 7/8in)

timber	origin	characteristics	common uses
Softwoods			
Parana pine	S. America	Pale yellow to dark brown with red streaks in heartwood. Close, straight grain. Often free of knots.	Joinery and light construction work.
Russian red deal	Baltic and Siberia	Honey to reddish brown colour. Regular grain, strong and easily worked.	Building and general construction work. Available in large sizes.
Sitka spruce	U.S.A. & Canada	Creamy white to pale brown. Strong, tough and straight grained.	Used for interior and exterior joinery. Obtainable in large sizes.
Western red cedar	N. America	Light yellow sapwood and pink to dark brown heartwood. Soft and easily worked but very durable.	Light construction work out of doors. Weather boarding, fencing and garden furniture. Available in large sizes.
Hardwoods			
Abura	W. Africa	Pale red to light brown. Fine, even texture and moderately hard.	Joinery and furniture making.
Ash	Europe	Pale fawn colour with dark streaks. Tough, close-grained with flexible quality.	Tool handles, shafts and turnery.
Beech	Europe	Pinkish colour with characteristic flecks. Straight grained, tough and durable.	Workshop equipment and domestic fittings. Furniture, toys and tool handles.
Elm	Europe	Dull brown with pale sapwood. Irregular grain.	Exterior work and turnery.
Mahogany (Honduras)	S. America	Rich reddish brown. Strong, close-grained and stable.	High quality furniture making.
Oak	Europe	Golden brown with pale sapwood. Strong, tough and durable. Silvery grain figure on quartered boards.	Furniture, construction work and flooring.
Oak	Japan	Softer with less prominent figure.	Furniture, construction work and flooring.
Sycamore	Europe	White, close-grained and strong. Can be worked to a high finish.	Often used in veneer form to achieve a colour contrast.
Walnut (African)	Africa	Golden brown with dark streaks. Regular grain and easy to work.	Furniture and interior joinery.

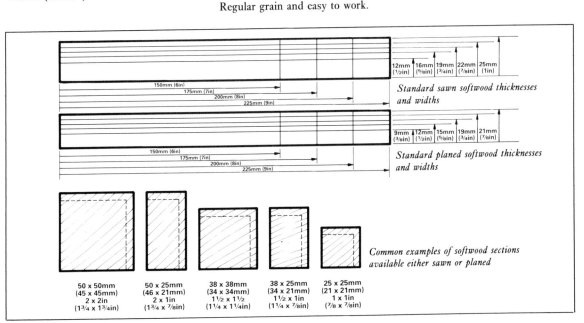

12mm (½in) 16mm (⅝in) 19mm (¾in) 22mm (⅞in) 25mm (1in)

150mm (6in) 175mm (7in) 200mm (8in) 225mm (9in)

Standard sawn softwood thicknesses and widths

9mm (⅜in) 12mm (½in) 15mm (⅝in) 19mm (¾in) 21mm (⅞in)

150mm (6in) 175mm (7in) 200mm (8in) 225mm (9in)

Standard planed softwood thicknesses and widths

Common examples of softwood sections available either sawn or planed

| 50 x 50mm (45 x 45mm) 2 x 2in (1¾ x 1¾in) | 50 x 25mm (46 x 21mm) 2 x 1in (1¾ x ⅞in) | 38 x 38mm (34 x 34mm) 1½ x 1½ (1¼ x 1¼in) | 38 x 25mm (34 x 21mm) 1½ x 1in (1¼ x ⅞in) | 25 x 25mm (21 x 21mm) 1 x 1in (⅞ x ⅞in) |

MANUFACTURED BOARD MATERIALS

There is a wide range of different plywoods available, giving a choice of timber from which it has been made, surface quality and appearance and suitability for different working conditions. The working conditions for which a plywood is suitable are decided not so much by the material from which it is made but by the adhesive which has been used to glue the veneers together. The suitability of plywoods to different working conditions is indicated by the following abbreviations:

INT – for interior use.
MR – moisture resistant.
WBP – weather and boilproof.

Plywoods are also graded to indicate the standard of surface quality, these gradings being A, B and BB.

Common plywood thicknesses are 4, 6, 9, 12, 15 and 18mm ($\frac{1}{8}$, $\frac{1}{4}$, $\frac{3}{8}$, $\frac{1}{2}$, $\frac{5}{8}$ and $\frac{3}{4}$in), and the most usual full sheet size is 2440 × 1220mm (96 × 48in). The strongest plywood for construction purposes is birch ply, which is completely made up of thin veneers. Other plywoods made of different timbers often have a different construction in which thin veneers are alternated with thicker veneers, and although this type of plywood is not as strong, it is cheaper. With the thinner plywoods there is again a choice of construction. A stronger plywood will have layers of about the same thickness, but a cheaper board, which is perfectly suitable for fitting into the backs of cupboards, may have a stout-heart construction. Plywood is also available with decorative veneers on one side in thicknesses of 4, 6, 9 and 12mm ($\frac{1}{8}$, $\frac{1}{4}$, $\frac{3}{8}$ and $\frac{1}{2}$in).

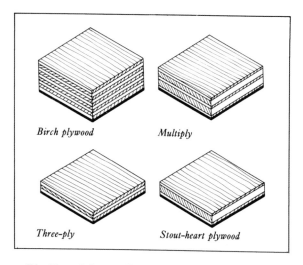

Birch plywood   *Multiply*

Three-ply   *Stout-heart plywood*

Blockboard is usually 18mm ($\frac{3}{4}$in) thick and has a veneer either side of softwood core strips. For high-class cabinet work where surfaces are to be veneered, laminboard should be considered as it is a more stable material and sometimes has a 5-layer construction. Standard blockboard is a good material for furniture

construction and the standard sheet size is 2440 × 1220mm (96 × 48in).

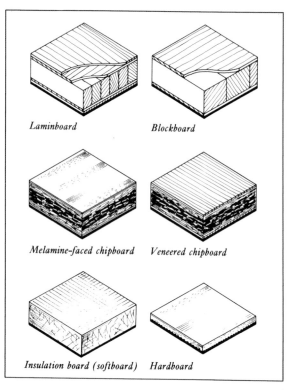

Laminboard   *Blockboard*

Melamine-faced chipboard   *Veneered chipboard*

Insulation board (softboard)   *Hardboard*

Plain chipboard is available in full sheets in thicknesses of 12, 15 and 18mm ($\frac{1}{2}$, $\frac{5}{8}$ and $\frac{3}{4}$in). Chipboard is most commonly used in the veneered or melamine-faced forms, and the thickness of these materials is 16mm ($\frac{5}{8}$in). The boards are normally stocked in 1m 830mm and 2m 440mm (72 and 96in) lengths and a full range of widths would include 152, 229, 305, 381, 457, 533 and 610mm (6, 9, 12, 15, 18, 21 and 24in). The melamine-faced boards are available in plain white or beige, or printed with a teak or pine pattern. The veneered boards are usually covered with a natural mahogany veneer or a natural pine veneer.

Insulation board (softboard) consists of wood fibres compressed and glued together, and at 12mm ($\frac{1}{2}$in) thick it can be a useful notice board or lining material. It is supplied in the standard sheet size of 2440 × 1220mm (96 × 48in) and is often painted a magnolia colour on one face. Hardboard is essentially the same material which has been further compressed to a thickness of 3.2mm ($\frac{1}{8}$in). Hardboard is ideal for fitting into the backs of cupboards, the bottoms of small drawers, the backings of pictures and a host of other uses. For some purposes it will be an advantage to obtain tempered hardboard which is impregnated with oil or resin to make it suitable for exterior use. Perforated hardboard (pegboard) is a further adaptation of the material which is often used for displays and has 4.8mm ($\frac{3}{16}$in) holes drilled at 19mm ($\frac{3}{4}$in) centres.

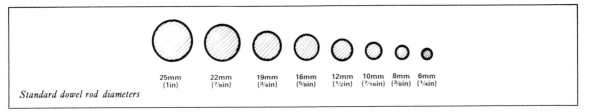

Standard dowel rod diameters

25mm (1in) 22mm (⁷⁄₈in) 19mm (³⁄₄in) 16mm (⁵⁄₈in) 12mm (¹⁄₂in) 10mm (⁷⁄₁₆in) 8mm (³⁄₈in) 6mm (¹⁄₄in)

Dowel rod is made of birch or ramin and is commonly available in 1m (39in) lengths. Occasionally 2m (78in) lengths can be found and these are less wasteful. The standard dowel diameters are 25, 22, 19, 16, 12, 10, 8 and 6mm ($1, \frac{7}{8}, \frac{3}{4}, \frac{5}{8}, \frac{1}{2}, \frac{3}{8}, \frac{5}{16}$ and $\frac{1}{4}$in), and it is an extremely useful constructional and jointing material.

Decorative veneers are priced per square metre or yard and are supplied in random widths, their thickness usually being about 1mm ($\frac{1}{16}$in). Thicker construction veneers which are useful for lamination work come in thicknesses of $1\frac{1}{2}$, 2 and 3mm ($\frac{1}{16}, \frac{3}{32}$ and $\frac{1}{8}$in) and are also charged per square metre or yard.

2 Planing timber to size

If the timber to be planed is rough sawn a face side must firstly be established. In choosing the side which will be the face side knots and blemishes should be avoided, as it is this which shows on the outside of the workpiece. The surface must be planed straight and true along its length and across its width. Thicker timber sections may be held in the bench vice but thinner pieces are planed on the bench top, working against the bench stop. The face side should be tested for true along its length and across its width with a straight edge before being marked with the accepted face side marking. (A steel rule can be used as a convenient straight edge for work on a small scale.)

The face edge is planed to be true along its length and square to the face side. In doing this a square corner is achieved from which the width and thickness required can be marked. The timber is held in the vice and a straight edge is again used to test for true. A try square is used to test for square and it should be noted that the stock of the try square is run along the face side for this. When the face edge is straight and square it is marked with the accepted face edge marking.

A marking gauge is used to set out the desired width, the stock of the gauge being run along the face edge. The gauge should be set to the correct measurement with a steel rule, taking care to measure to the point of the spur. The gauge thumbscrew should be lightly tightened and the measurement checked, as movement sometimes takes place. The gauge can be tapped lightly to adjust to the exact measurement, the thumbscrew then being finally tightened. When using the gauge it should be held in such a way that the spur is dragged behind. This will decrease the possibility of the spur following the grain rather than making a clear line on the wood. Gauge lines should be made on both sides of the material and the waste planed off, taking care to arrive at both gauge lines at the same time. If this is done it will ensure that the planed surface is square.

With the marking gauge set to the required thickness, the timber is marked out on both sides by running the gauge along the face side. The waste material is again planed away to the gauge lines, with the timber resting on the bench top against the stop.

PLANING END GRAIN (*see over*)

When planing end grain there is a danger of splitting the wood where there is no support for the grain. There are a number of ways of overcoming this problem and the method used will depend on the size of the timber being planed and the equipment available. To ensure a clean surface a knife line should always be made to plane to and the plane blade should have a sharp edge and be set finely to cut only a little with each stroke.

The most common method is to plane towards a piece of scrapwood which is placed in the vice with the workpiece to support the far edge. The principle behind this method is that the scrapwood may split but the workpiece will not. It is important that the scrapwood strip is parallel-sided and that both the workpiece and scrapwood are set low in the vice, to prevent movement or vibration.

An alternative method is to remove the far corner of the material which is where the splitting is likely to occur. The corner is removed by planing upwards at an angle of about 45° making a chamfer down to the depth of the knife line.

When working with wide material the splitting problem can be avoided by planing towards the centre from both sides. In this way the plane will not pass over any end grain that is not supported. An alternative method for wide boards is to cramp a scrapwood strip on the far end with a sash cramp, the bench vice being used to hold the board upright.

If a shooting board is available or can be made it provides an excellent way of planing square ends on fairly narrow material. The board has a block mounted on it which holds the material at 90° to the plane and supports the end grain. As the plane is pushed up and down the trough in the board, on its side, the material is pushed out against the plane and in this way cuts are made until the knife line is reached. Shooting boards can be made for planing angles other than 90°, and a 45° mitre shooting board can be a useful piece of equipment for jobs such as picture framing. Note the batten fixed to the underside of the shooting board to allow it to be held in the vice, and also the chamfered corner which prevents waste material throwing the plane off course.

BENCH PLANES (*see over*)

The size or model of bench plane that is chosen for a particular task is very important. The three common sizes of bench plane are the smoothing plane (225–

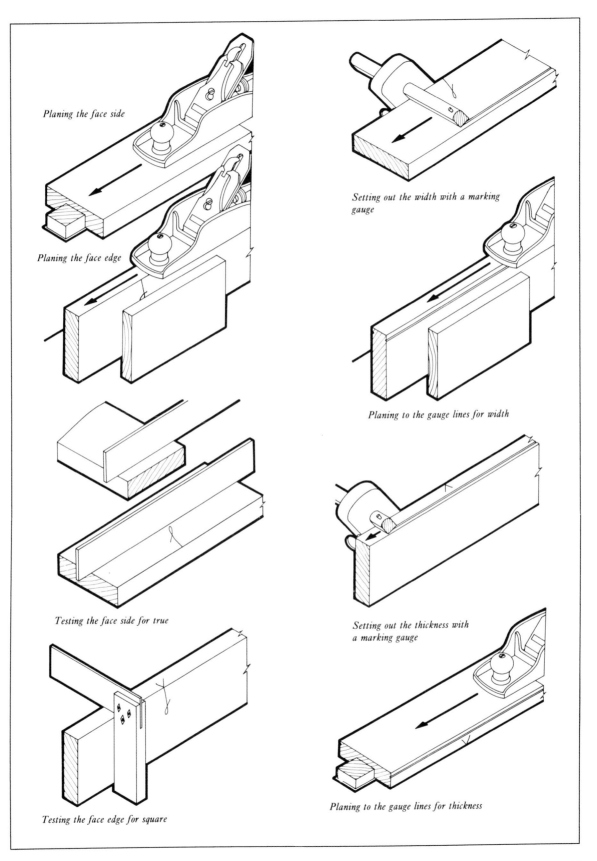

Planing the face side

Planing the face edge

Testing the face side for true

Testing the face edge for square

Setting out the width with a marking gauge

Planing to the gauge lines for width

Setting out the thickness with a marking gauge

Planing to the gauge lines for thickness

13

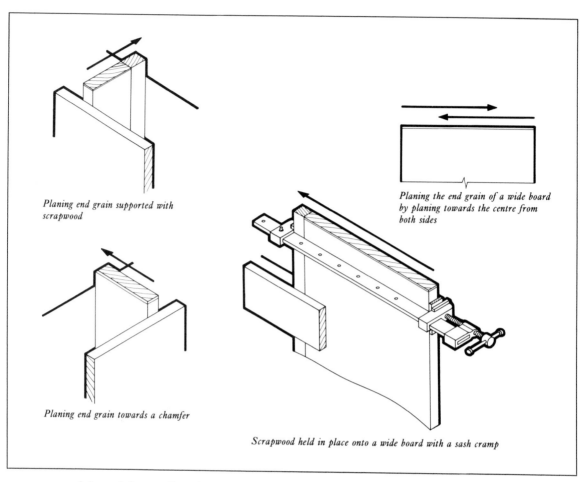

Planing end grain supported with
scrapwood

Planing the end grain of a wide board
by planing towards the centre from
both sides

Planing end grain towards a chamfer

Scrapwood held in place onto a wide board with a sash cramp

250mm, 9–10in) used for small scale work and for finishing, the jack plane (350–425mm, 14–17in) used for larger work and for removing waste quickly and the try plane (450–600mm, 18–24in) which is used for long edges and surfaces. The principle of the plane is that the accurately ground flat sole will remove the high spots from a timber surface to bring it into true. To be able to do this the plane must be long enough to bridge the

hollows on the surface and consequently the longer the workpiece, the longer the plane itself should be.

The adjustment of the plane is also crucial, and there is a simple sequence which can be followed to achieve the correct setting. Firstly, the blade should be wound out, by turning the adjustment wheel clockwise, until it can be seen when looking along the sole of the plane from the toe, with the plane upside down. The lateral

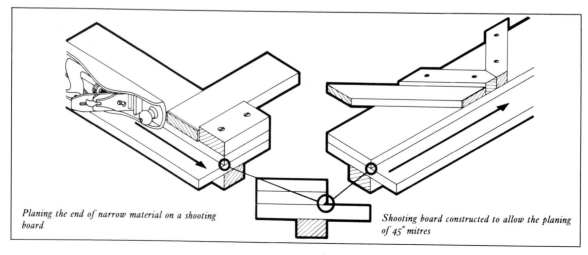

Planing the end of narrow material on a shooting
board

Shooting board constructed to allow the planing
of 45° mitres

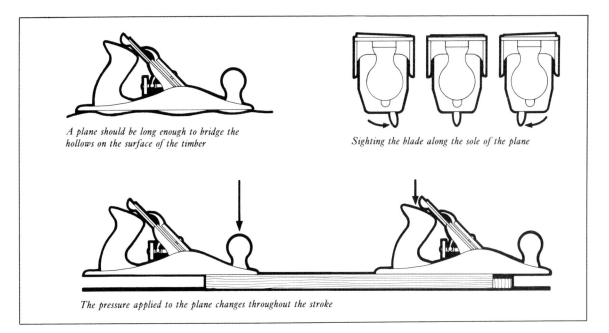

A plane should be long enough to bridge the hollows on the surface of the timber

Sighting the blade along the sole of the plane

The pressure applied to the plane changes throughout the stroke

adjustment lever, above the handle, is then used to position the blade so that it is protruding by the same amount right across its width. The blade is then completely withdrawn by turning the adjustment wheel anti-clockwise, and then brought out again until it can just be seen by turning the wheel clockwise again. The plane should now be tried on the timber and the depth of cut can be increased if necessary. It is important that the final adjustment should always be made by turning the wheel clockwise as this takes up all the slack in the lever mechanism.

To ensure a true surface when planing timber, the pressure applied to the plane when pushing it along should shift throughout the stroke. To begin the stroke the pressure is required at the front of the plane to keep it in line with the timber surface, and for the same reason at the end of the stroke this pressure is required at the back of the plane.

When it is necessary to hold small square material at an angle which will allow the corners to be planed, to produce an octagonal section or to prepare the material for the lathe, the cradle is a useful piece of equipment which can easily be made in the workshop.

Portable planing machines can make the dressing of rough sawn timber considerably easier but they are probably best suited to work on a fairly large scale. Some models have the particularly desirable facility of being able to cut rebates to precise settings.

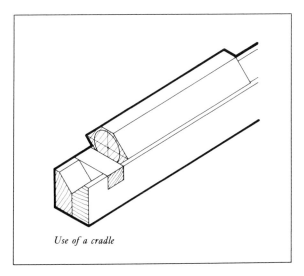

Use of a cradle

Portable planing machine

3 The use of dowel for jointing

Dowel rod is widely used for jointing purposes, both by industry and the handyman. The use of dowels to reinforce other types of joint is a practice which is centuries old – for example, the pegging of a tenon – but it is now common to use dowel as the complete joint. The attraction of using dowel is the ease of preparation as compared with the more traditional jointing methods, whilst a strong joint is still achieved. Dowels can be used in a wide variety of situations, e.g. corner joints between legs and rails, edge to edge joints and corner joints in slab constructions.

Dowels can be bought which are prepared for immediate use in various lengths and diameters, but it is obviously cheaper to prepare dowels from lengths of dowel rod. If it is essential that the dowels be made from a particular timber for strength or decorative purposes a dowel plate will be needed. A narrow section of the wood to be used is driven through one of the larger holes in the plate and then driven through the holes in sequence until the required diameter is achieved. A dowel which is to be used for jointing should have slight chamfers at both ends and should be grooved along its length. The chamfer allows for easy location into the holes during assembly and also gives glue space inside the joint. (The holes into which the dowels are to be fitted should be lightly countersunk for the same reasons.) The groove allows the escape of surplus glue from the holes. If only a few dowels are being prepared they can be marked out for length and sawn on a sawing board and the groove cut with a back saw, whilst pinching the dowel in the corner of the vice. Where a number of dowels of the same size are required there are various techniques which can be used to quicken the process.

To make the groove a length of dowel can be driven through a wooden block which has a hole drilled through it that is slightly larger than the diameter of the dowel rod. A nail is driven into the block so that it protrudes into the central bore and it is the point of the nail which makes the groove as the dowel passes. The dowels should be cut to a length which is 2 or 3mm (about $\frac{1}{8}$in) less than the total depth of the two holes into which they will fit. This is to ensure that the joint comes fully together and to allow glue space at the bottom of the holes. Once again a wooden block can be used to simplify the process. The block is drilled to allow the dowel to pass easily through it; the length of dowel required is marked from the end of the block and a saw cut made to go through to the central bore. With the block held on a sawing board, or in a vice, the dowel rod which has previously been grooved is pushed through the block and sawn off when the end is flush with the end of the block. In this way any number can be cut to exactly the same length.

A dowel trimmer bit fitted into a carpenter's brace may be found useful to make the chamfers on the ends of the dowels, but this can be carried out equally well with a file or glasspaper.

When making dowelled joints it is most important to drill the holes in exactly the right position and conse-

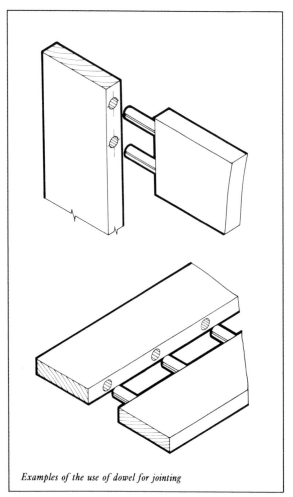

Examples of the use of dowel for jointing

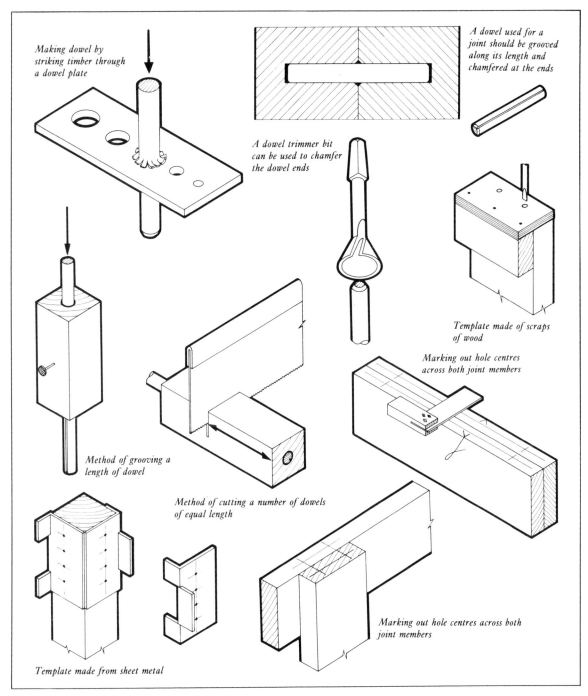

Making dowel by striking timber through a dowel plate

A dowel used for a joint should be grooved along its length and chamfered at the ends

A dowel trimmer bit can be used to chamfer the dowel ends

Template made of scraps of wood

Marking out hole centres across both joint members

Method of grooving a length of dowel

Method of cutting a number of dowels of equal length

Marking out hole centres across both joint members

Template made from sheet metal

quently the marking of the hole centres is critical. When the same arrangement of holes is to be drilled a number of times it is worth spending some time in preparing a template or jig which will aid the marking out of the hole centres. These are easily made from scraps of plywood or sheet metal and should be prepared so that the centres can be accurately marked with a bradawl or awl. Accuracy can sometimes be achieved by marking out across both joint members whilst they are held together in a vice or cramp. To do this whenever possible will both save time and help towards a successful joint.

A further method of ensuring the accurate location of dowel holes is to use dowel locators when making edge joints or wide corner joints. The locators are pushed into the edge of one board in the required positions along a centre line and the second board is placed in position against the first and pressure applied. In this way the protruding points on the locators will accurately mark the centres for the holes onto the second board.

There is available on the market a number of drilling jigs to aid the drilling of straight holes but again a jig can be easily prepared in most cases, using fairly thick timber to guide the drill. Such a jig may take the form of a strip of timber nailed to the edge of a board through which the dowel holes are drilled, and indeed such a system may eliminate the need to mark the hole centres at all. Wherever possible the use of a pillar drill will guarantee the straightness and depth of the holes. In the absence of any kind of aid it can be helpful first to drill a pilot hole of about half of the dowel diameter for the final drill to follow. The depth of the hole can be marked onto the drill with tape, or with a piece of rubber tube or cork. Once the holes have been drilled they should be lightly countersunk, as previously explained.

The corner butt joint can be strengthened by dowelling and this is usually done with the dowels hidden in blind holes. However, a feature of the joint can be made by taking the dowels right the way through from the outside.

Provided that the dowel holes are at right angles to the joint surface, dowelled joints can be made at any angle and a common example of this is the dowelled mitre joint. It should be mentioned here that joints of this nature are difficult to cramp up and cramping blocks may need to be glued onto the joint members, to be removed after assembly.

Dowels are commonly used to join legs and rails in frame constructions for tables and chairs and there can be a problem of the dowels meeting inside the leg if two rails meet the leg at the same level. This will result in the dowels having to be shorter than the length that is really required for sufficient strength. To solve this problem the positions of the dowels in the rails can be staggered so that they pass each other inside the leg and can achieve full length.

As a guide to the size of dowel that should be used for a joint the dowel diameter should be approximately half of the thickness of the timber, e.g. 20mm ($\frac{3}{4}$in) timber/ 10mm ($\frac{3}{8}$in) dowel, etc.

A length of dowel can be used to allow screws to be driven into end grain. The grip of a screw relies on the threads moving between the wood fibres and consequently there is very little strength in a screw which is driven into end grain. A length of dowel fitted into a hole which has been drilled in the appropriate place will provide a section of grain which is in the correct direction for a screw to gain grip.

As a reinforcement dowel rod is most commonly used with the mortise and tenon and halving joints. The drawbore tenon is particularly useful when a frame is being constructed which is too large for normal cramps. The joint has holes drilled through the mortise and the tenon but the centres of these holes are marked so that, as the dowel is driven through, the tenon is pulled firmly into the mortise. To help with this movement the end of the dowel should be tapered.

Dowel rod can also be used as a constructional material in its own right, usually as a spacer or stretcher between side or end panels. In these situations the dowel can be fitted into blind holes or have a shoulder, formed by reducing the diameter at the end or by fitting a piece of smaller diameter dowel. For even greater strength the dowel can be taken through at its full diameter and a wedge fitted from the outside. It should be noted that the wedge which is driven into a sawn slot in the end of the dowel must lie across the grain of a solid wood panel.

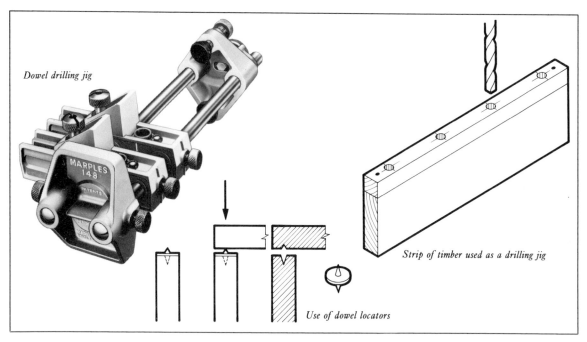

Dowel drilling jig

Strip of timber used as a drilling jig

Use of dowel locators

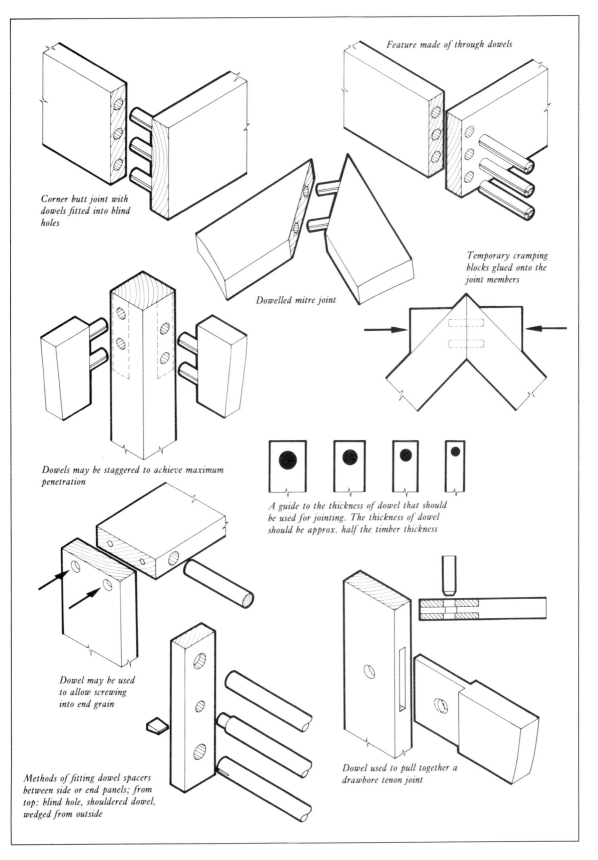

Corner butt joint with dowels fitted into blind holes

Feature made of through dowels

Dowelled mitre joint

Temporary cramping blocks glued onto the joint members

Dowels may be staggered to achieve maximum penetration

A guide to the thickness of dowel that should be used for jointing. The thickness of dowel should be approx. half the timber thickness

Dowel may be used to allow screwing into end grain

Methods of fitting dowel spacers between side or end panels; from top: blind hole, shouldered dowel, wedged from outside

Dowel used to pull together a drawbore tenon joint

4 Halving joints

As their name suggests, halving joints are those where half of the thickness of the joint members is removed so that when the joint is assembled the sides are flush. These joints are mainly used in the construction of frameworks where members meet or cross and are easy to mark out and cut, although their ultimate strength depends on accurate cutting.

Where a cross member meets the outside of a frame the tee halving can be used. To mark out this joint a shoulder line is firstly marked on the cross member at a distance of the width of the material plus 2mm ($\frac{3}{32}$in) from the end. This extra material will allow the joint to be planed flush after assembly and should be allowed for when cutting the frame members to length. A gauge line is the simplest way of marking the depth of the joint along both sides and across the end of the cross member. (It is very difficult to set a gauge precisely by measurement and a useful technique to ensure that the gauge is

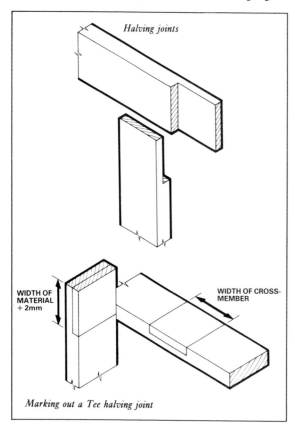

Marking out a Tee halving joint

set exactly to half of the thickness is as follows: set the gauge to an approximation of the measurement and make a light mark on the timber from one face and then from the opposite face. If the two marks do not coincide then the gauge is adjusted accordingly and the procedure repeated until the marks exactly coincide.) The width of the cross member is marked out exactly between two knife lines onto the outside frame member and these lines are taken over the edges so that a gauge can be used again to mark out the depth of the joint.

The waste material on the end of the cross member is removed by following the sawing sequence shown. The saw cut down the length of the material is made in three stages, sawing to the waste side of the line but only just leaving the lines in. The waste is then finally released by sawing across the shoulder line whilst the timber is held firmly onto a sawing board. A useful technique here, especially when working on wide timber, is to make a shallow cut up to the shoulder line with a chisel to locate the saw in the correct position whilst the cut is established.

The waste material on the outside frame member is released by sawing across the grain at either end of the marking, with the timber held onto a sawing board. It is sometimes useful to make further sawcuts to divide the waste and allow better control when chiselling it away. The waste is removed by chiselling up towards the centre from both sides and to depth, and then levelled by horizontal paring. This work is best carried out with a fairly wide chisel and the workpiece should be held firmly in the vice. At this stage the joint can be tested for fit and trimmed as necessary. If two frame members meet at an angle other than 90° the tee halving can be adapted to suit.

In situations where a cross member has to resist a strong pulling force there are two variations of the dovetail halving which are able to resist such a force due to their shape. Both the dovetail halving and barefaced dovetail halving are marked out with a slope of approximately 1 in 7; a sliding bevel would be useful in cases where a number of holes is to be marked out. The dovetailed end of the cross member should be marked out first in a similar manner to that just described for the tee halving, the sloped corner, or corners, being removed last. The waste material which is to be cut from the outside frame member is marked out by tracing around the dovetail whilst it is held in the correct

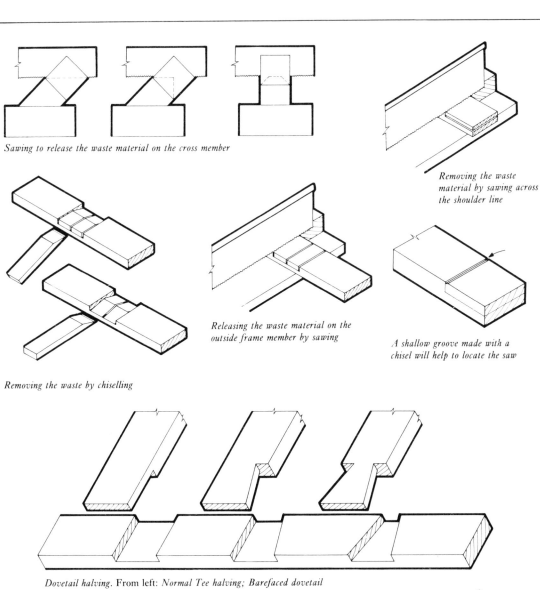

Sawing to release the waste material on the cross member

Removing the waste material by sawing across the shoulder line

Releasing the waste material on the outside frame member by sawing

A shallow groove made with a chisel will help to locate the saw

Removing the waste by chiselling

Dovetail halving. From left: Normal Tee halving; Barefaced dovetail halving; dovetail halving

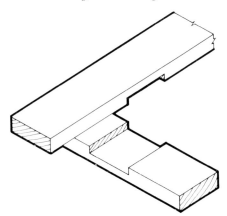

The cross-halving cut across the width of the material

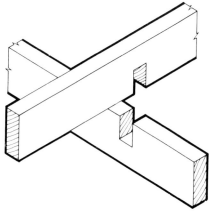

The cross-halving cut across the thickness of the material

21

position. The removal of this waste is carried out by the same procedure as that for the tee halving.

When two members cross at right angles to one another the cross halving is practically the only joint which can be used and it may be cut across the width or the thickness of the material. In both cases exactly half should be taken from each piece, the waste being removed by sawing and chiselling. There is also an elaboration of the cross halving which can be used to give greater strength and a neater appearance.

If the appearance of the frame is of paramount importance and no great strength is required, the mitred corner halving may be appropriate. This joint can also be adapted to take a rebate from the back if a panel is to be fitted.

Although it is not strictly a halving joint the lap or rebate joint is included here as an extremely versatile jointing method for box and carcase construction. This joint enjoys the advantages of being simple to cut and yet has a good appearance and strength. In addition, it is also able to accommodate rebates and grooves.

The sloping halving may be appropriate if a required length is having to be constructed by joining two pieces end to end. A range of joints for this purpose is dealt with in the section on lengthening and widening joints, but the sloping halving is adequate if no great strength is required.

A major disadvantage of halvings is that a form of holding or fixing is often necessary to hold the two sides of the joint together when assembling a frame. If the joints are only to be glued then a G-cramp can be used for this, but it may more often be the case that nails, pins or screws are used to achieve it.

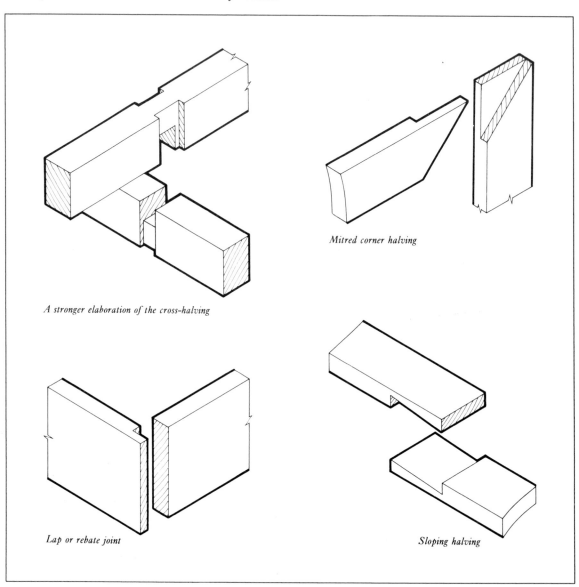

A stronger elaboration of the cross-halving

Mitred corner halving

Lap or rebate joint

Sloping halving

5 Mortise and tenon joints

The mortise and tenon joint has many variations and as a result is extremely versatile and widely used. The basic principle of the joint allows both strength and neat appearance, and once the cutting procedure is understood the joint is perhaps easier to make than it may appear. The joint is mostly used to construct frameworks. These may be flat frames which have been grooved or rebated to take a wooden panel or glass, or three-dimensional frames which form the underframe to a chair or table.

The joint is shown in its simplest forms by the square haunched mortise and tenon and the common or plain mortise and tenon. The haunched tenon is necessary at a frame corner and it is a means of providing full support across the width of the rail whilst still firmly locating the tenon from the top. The tenon should be approximately one-third of the thickness of the rail and may pass right through the stile or leg, or for the sake of appearance may be stopped about two-thirds of the way inside the material. To mark out the tenon a shoulder line is marked with a knife and try square all around the rail at the required distance from the end. If the tenon is to go right through the stile or leg it is advisable to add 2mm ($\frac{3}{32}$in) or so to the length of the tenon to allow it to be planed flush after assembly, and this should be included when cutting the rails to length. A mortise gauge is then set to the width of the chisel which will be used to cut the mortise. The stock of the gauge is adjusted so that the parallel lines are marked in the centre of the rail. (Again, to do this by measurement is very difficult and it is easier to set the gauge at an estimate and then make marks from both faces of the rail. If the marks do not coincide the gauge should be adjusted slightly and the exercise repeated. When the marks coincide the gauge must be accurately set.) The gauge is then used to mark the width of the tenon across the end of the rail and down both sides to the shoulder line. This is all the marking that is necessary for the plain mortise and tenon, but if the joint being made has a square or sloping haunch or is shouldered these features should be marked on. There are guidelines to the relative proportions of these features which allow their dimensions to be worked out.

To mark out the mortise, pencil lines are squared across the material to show the full width of the rail in the appropriate position. Shoulders and haunch spaces should be marked out in a similar way. When cutting a haunched mortise and tenon at the end of a stile or leg it

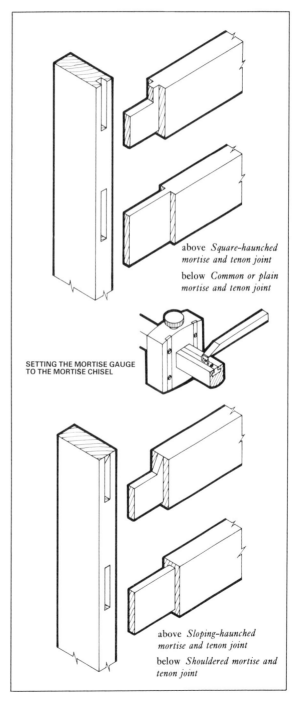

above *Square-haunched mortise and tenon joint*

below *Common or plain mortise and tenon joint*

SETTING THE MORTISE GAUGE TO THE MORTISE CHISEL

above *Sloping-haunched mortise and tenon joint*

below *Shouldered mortise and tenon joint*

It is possible for two tenons to meet inside a leg at the same level, without any loss of strength, using either mitred tenons or interlocking tenons. When making these joints there is a danger of weakening the leg through poor positioning of the mortises. The simplest solution is to move the mortises out towards the outer faces of the leg, but if the rail is to remain in a central position relative to the leg the tenon should be set off-centre on the rail.

The forked tenon and the twin tenon are also joint adaptations to prevent weakness in a joint. The forked tenon is used when a wide rail is to be jointed and the division of the tenon into two reduces the amount of material that has to be removed from the stile, thus preventing weakness. The double or twin tenon is used when thick material is to be jointed, once again to prevent weakness. When a tenon is taken right the way through the material there is the further option of securing the joint with wedges, making it difficult to pull the joint apart. The wedged tenon is parallel-sided but is fitted into a mortise which tapers slightly towards the outer face. When the joint has been glued and assembled the wedges are driven into the openings left by the tapered mortise. The wedges and tenon are sawn and planed flush after the glue has set. An alternative method of wedging is to drive the wedges into sawcuts made in the tenon. Once again, the mortise is slightly tapered to accept the movement caused by the wedges. The wedges needed for this type of operation are normally prepared by sawing a board of the correct thickness as shown.

Where an upright is jointed to a flat base, e.g. a lamp base, the stub tenon is a simple joint to cut. The square tenon is shouldered all round and is fitted into a square mortise cut through the flat board.

The pegged tenon is a decorative joint which is often used as a means of joining a stretcher rail to the upright supports of a bench or table. The rail passes through a mortise and in turn has a mortise in itself to accept a tapered peg. To allow for tightening the mortise in, the rail should have spare length inside the upright and the outer edge of the mortise should be tapered to match the taper on the peg.

The barefaced tenon is often used in gate and fence construction where boarding is to be nailed to rails but must not protrude beyond the fence posts or gate stiles. The single shoulder allows a greater strength of tenon and also allows the mortise to be placed centrally in the post or stile.

If a large framework is being constructed and the use of cramps is impractical or impossible, the drawbore tenon can be very useful. Holes are drilled through the mortise and the tenon on slightly different centres so that when the dowel is driven through it pulls the joint tightly together.

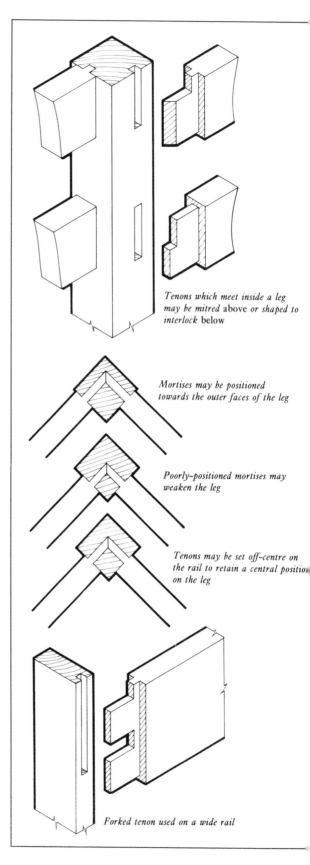

Tenons which meet inside a leg may be mitred above or shaped to interlock below

Mortises may be positioned towards the outer faces of the leg

Poorly-positioned mortises may weaken the leg

Tenons may be set off-centre on the rail to retain a central position on the leg

Forked tenon used on a wide rail

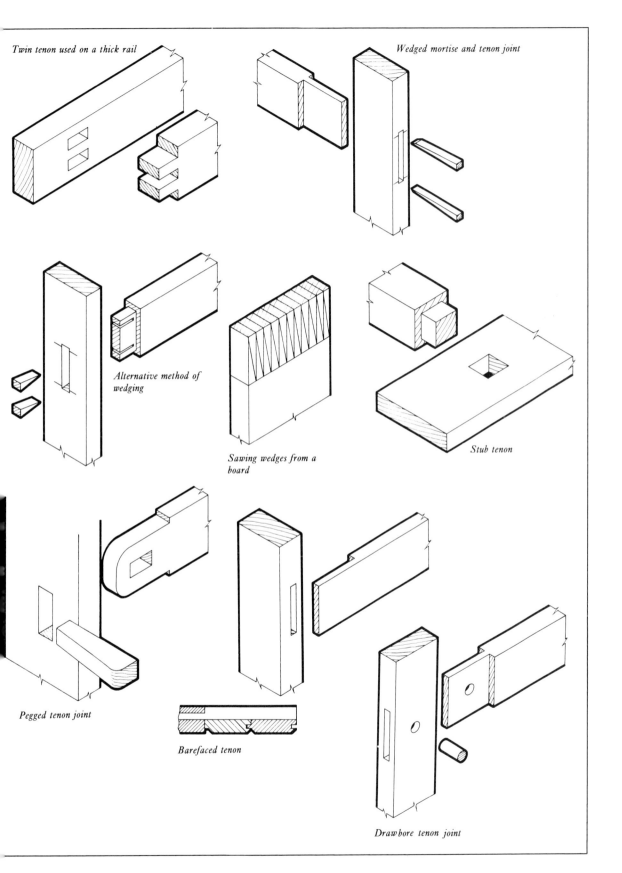

Twin tenon used on a thick rail

Wedged mortise and tenon joint

Alternative method of wedging

Sawing wedges from a board

Stub tenon

Pegged tenon joint

Barefaced tenon

Drawbore tenon joint

27

6 Bridle joints

Bridle joints are effective joints for framework constructions where the load is not excessive. Such frames may be cupboard doors, the skeletal frame of a cabinet or a frame to hold a picture or mirror. The main disadvantage of bridle joints is that the end grain is apparent and for this reason they tend to be used if appearance is not important or if the outside edges are not seen.

There are many variations of the joint but the basic form of the bridle is shown in the corner bridle. The thickness of the material is divided into thirds and on one joint member the central section is removed to form an open mortise and on the second member the two cheeks are removed to leave a central tenon. In reality, the thickness of the central tenon is often dictated by the size of the chisel which will be used to complete the open mortise slot; this chisel being the closest for width to a third of the material thickness.

The first step in the marking out of the joint is to pencil in the shoulder lines on both joint members at a distance of the width of the material plus 2mm ($\frac{3}{32}$in). This extra material will allow the joint to be planed flush after assembly and should be taken into account when cutting the frame members to length. A mortise gauge set to mark out a central section equal in width to the chosen chisel, exactly in the centre, is the best tool for marking across the ends of the joint members and down to the shoulder lines on both sides. When the waste material has been marked by shading, the shoulder lines should be marked with a knife where they are to be cut.

The cuts down the grain are each made in three stages with a backsaw as shown. The cheeks on either side of the tenon are removed by sawing across the shoulder lines whilst the wood is held firmly on a sawing board. The waste from the open mortise is removed with a chisel and mallet working from both sides to ensure a clean shoulder line. If the timber is fairly narrow most of this waste can be removed with a coping saw, before chiselling.

If a frame has a supporting cross member the Tee bridle can be utilised. The open mortise cut into the end of the cross member is made by the method previously described. The waste from the outer frame member is released by sawing across the width of the timber whilst the work is held on a sawing board. The waste is then removed by chiselling up towards the centre and to depth from both sides and finally levelled by horizontal paring. Greater control of this removal can be achieved by further sawcuts across the member to segment the waste.

If a shaped frame is being constructed both the corner or tee bridles can be made at angles other than 90°. Such oblique bridles are often the most sound solution to the problem of jointing at an irregular angle.

When a frame is to be viewed from the front, the mitred corner bridle would be most appropriate, e.g. a mirror frame. The cutting of this joint involves the same principles as those already covered, but obviously the marking out involves the use of a mitre square. If a

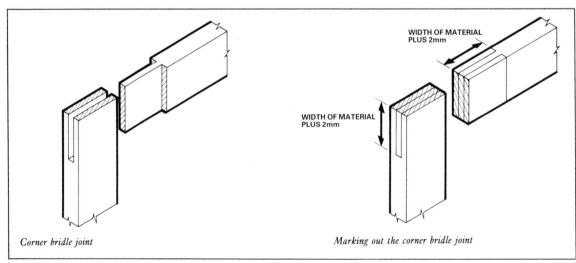

WIDTH OF MATERIAL PLUS 2mm

WIDTH OF MATERIAL PLUS 2mm

Corner bridle joint   *Marking out the corner bridle joint*

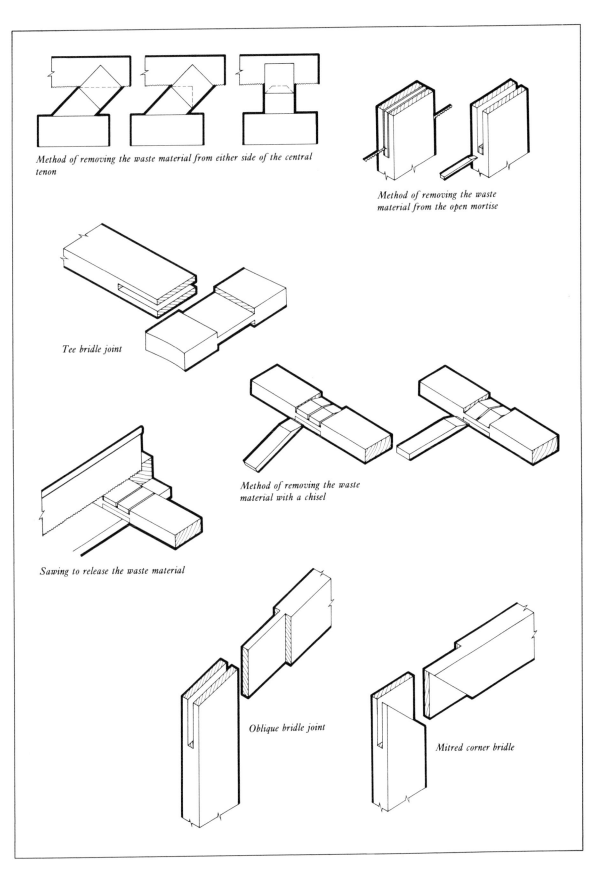

Method of removing the waste material from either side of the central tenon

Method of removing the waste material from the open mortise

Tee bridle joint

Method of removing the waste material with a chisel

Sawing to release the waste material

Oblique bridle joint

Mitred corner bridle

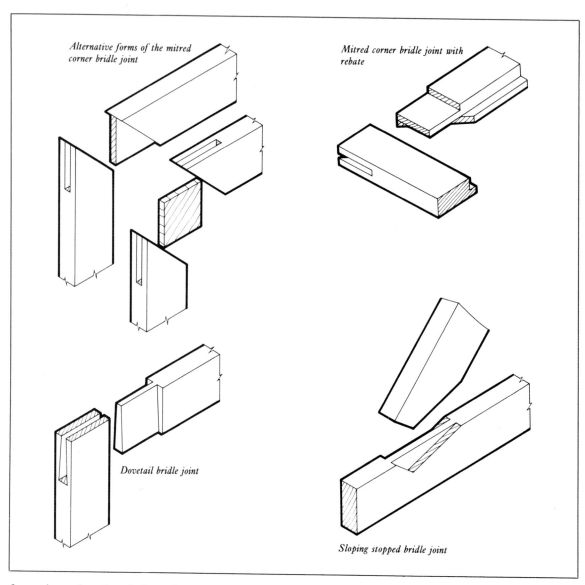

Alternative forms of the mitred corner bridle joint

Mitred corner bridle joint with rebate

Dovetail bridle joint

Sloping stopped bridle joint

frame is to be viewed from both sides there are variations of the mitred corner bridle which should perhaps be considered, but neither of these alternatives would be as strong as the standard form. The mitred corner bridle is useful for picture or mirror frames and in such situations will require a rebate from the back. The joint is easily adapted to take a rebate provided that the depth coincides with the measurements of the joint itself. Consequently the rebate should be either one-third or two-thirds of the thickness of the material deep.

In situations where a frame constructed with bridle joints is going to be under a considerable load the dovetail bridle should be considered for the corner joints. Although more difficult to cut it will be appreciated that the dovetail shaping on the central tenon enables it to resist any downward force. Once the joint has been marked out the cutting procedure is in

fact the same as that for the normal bridles.

If an oblique cross member is to be fitted within a frame, or a corner strut is to be fitted inside an L-shaped frame, the sloping stopped bridle can be used. The design of the joint means that little is taken away from the outer frame member and yet when the strut is in place an enormous strength advantage is gained. After marking, the joint is cut by chiselling from both sides down towards the centre.

When assembling bridle joints all surfaces that come into contact should be glued, and as the glueing area within the joints is large this should be the only form of fixing required. Care should be taken, however, when cramping up the joints as pressure is required from both directions, and in such situations it can be difficult to achieve accurate location.

7 Housing joints

Housing joints are most commonly used to fit shelves into cabinets or bookcases. The joints need not be confined to the horizontal plane however, and in the vertical plane they can be used to hold partitions and dividers. There are a variety of forms of the housing, but the essential principle of the joint is that the end of a shelf or partition is housed and held into a trench or groove cut into the outer member. The depth of this trench should be at least one-third of the thickness of the timber and no more than half of the thickness.

The joint in its simplest form is the through housing which, although strong, has the disadvantage that the joint is visible from both sides. This may not be important if the appearance of the article is not crucial or if some form of moulding or lipping is to be applied. A further method of disguising the joint is shown in the drawing where the shelf is made wider than the supporting side piece. The housing is marked in the correct position with knife lines, to a width which is equal to the thickness of the shelf or partition to be fitted. These lines are taken over the edges of the timber so that the depth of the housing can be marked with a marking gauge. In situations where shelves or dividers are to be housed at both ends, the positions of the housings should be marked across both boards laid together to ensure exact alignment.

The waste material is released by sawing to the waste side of the lines with a backsaw. Narrow timber can be held on a sawing board for this but wider boards will need to be cramped to the bench top. With wider boards it will also be necessary to cramp a piece of timber with a straight edge in position to guide the saw. A chisel which is slightly narrower than the housing itself is used to remove the waste, and firstly the ends are removed by chiselling up towards the centre and to depth. The main body of the waste is then removed by careful horizontal paring, working towards the centre from both sides. On wider boards a long paring chisel will be necessary to reach to the centre of the board and a router plane will be helpful in finishing the housing to depth (see photo 3 in Ch. 10).

If the joint is to be hidden from the front the stopped housing joint can be used. This is also the joint which would be used if the shelf were narrower than the side panel. As a guide, the housing is usually stopped by a distance equal to the thickness of the timber being fitted. The back of the joint remains the same as the

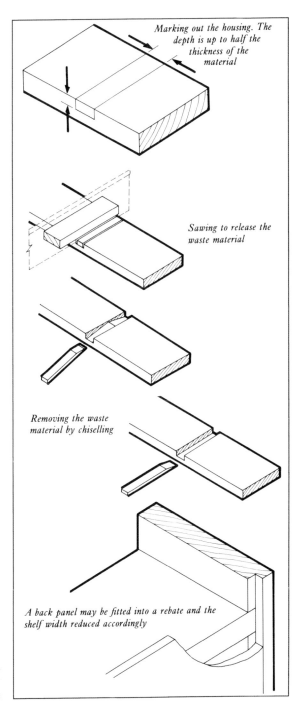

Marking out the housing. The depth is up to half the thickness of the material

Sawing to release the waste material

Removing the waste material by chiselling

A back panel may be fitted into a rebate and the shelf width reduced accordingly

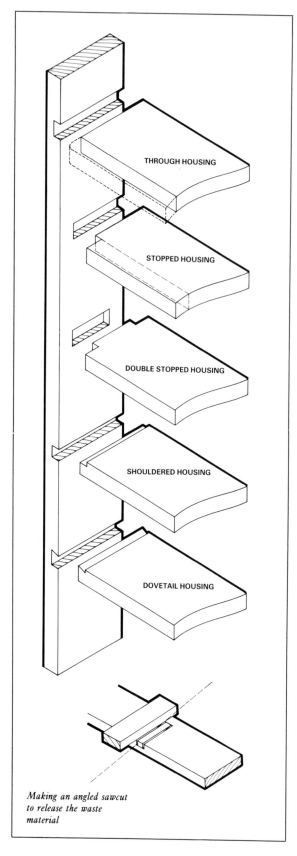

THROUGH HOUSING

STOPPED HOUSING

DOUBLE STOPPED HOUSING

SHOULDERED HOUSING

DOVETAIL HOUSING

Making an angled sawcut to release the waste material

through housing and a rebate can be cut if a back panel is to be fitted, the width of the shelf being reduced accordingly. The cutting procedure for the stopped housing is rather different and more difficult than for the through housing. The amount of sawing that can be done to release the waste material is limited to an angled sawcut. The stopped end of the housing then has to be chiselled, or drilled and chiselled away, to depth to allow for the movement of the nose of the saw as the sawing of the sides of the housing is completed. (A forstner bit is best for this drilling.) The waste material can only be chiselled away from the one side on a stopped housing and a router plane will be particularly useful to level the housing to depth. To fit into the housing the shelf or partition must have its front corner removed and this is easily achieved by sawing to cut lines.

If the joint is to be seen from both sides as in a shelved room divider, the double stopped housing can be used. This is most easily cut by drilling a complete row of holes to depth and by vertical chiselling, using mallet blows, to release the waste. The waste can then be removed by careful paring from the centre outwards, running the chisel along its grinding bevel. A straight edge cramped in place will help to achieve straight sides to the housing and a router plane can be used to finish it to depth.

The difficulty in cutting housings is to cut the trench to the correct width so that the shelf or partition fits without a gap. If there is sufficient thickness to the material the shouldered housing can be used to overcome this problem. The shoulder should be 3mm ($\frac{1}{8}$in) or so deep and can be incorporated into any of the housing joints previously mentioned. On narrow boards the shoulder can be sawn but on wide boards the use of a rebate plane would be advisable. (The plane would be working across the grain and should be set accordingly.)

The dovetail housing is difficult to cut but it has the great advantage of tying together the sides of the cabinet, resisting any tendency they might have to bow outwards. The dovetail housing can be through or stopped and the cutting procedures are the same as those previously described apart from the need to saw one side of the trench at an angle. This is most easily achieved by planing a wooden straight edge to the appropriate angle and cramping it in place as a sawing guide. The corresponding dovetail on the shelf can be made by firstly cutting a rebate by saw or rebate plane, and then opening it out to the correct angle with a chisel.

Where strength is at a premium the housing joint can be adapted to incorporate tenons. The double stopped housing with tenons might be found in a wall cabinet which has to take a particularly heavy load. The tenons may be stopped, or taken through to the outside, which will give the further option of wedging for even greater strength. To cut this joint the double stopped housing is cut first and the mortises are chiselled from the bottom of the housing.

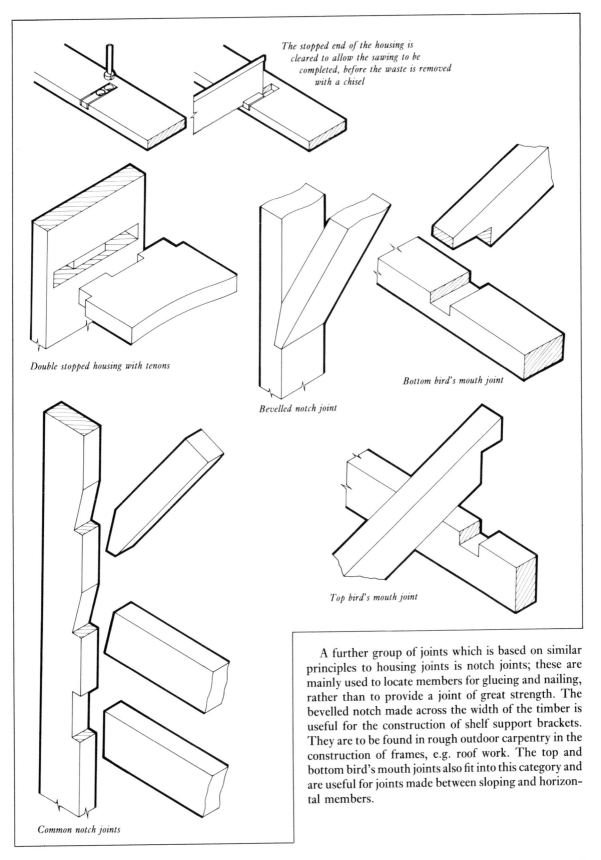

The stopped end of the housing is cleared to allow the sawing to be completed, before the waste is removed with a chisel

Double stopped housing with tenons

Bevelled notch joint

Bottom bird's mouth joint

Top bird's mouth joint

Common notch joints

A further group of joints which is based on similar principles to housing joints is notch joints; these are mainly used to locate members for glueing and nailing, rather than to provide a joint of great strength. The bevelled notch made across the width of the timber is useful for the construction of shelf support brackets. They are to be found in rough outdoor carpentry in the construction of frames, e.g. roof work. The top and bottom bird's mouth joints also fit into this category and are useful for joints made between sloping and horizontal members.

8 Dovetail joints

The dovetail joint is often rejected in favour of alternative joints which are considered to be easier to accomplish. In fact, the dovetail is not so difficult to cut as it may seem, but the working out of a measurement scheme and the marking out do demand patience. The dovetail is used in its various forms for all scales of box or carcase construction, from small jewellery boxes to the corner joints of cabinets.

There are general rules which can be applied to help with the calculation of a measurement scheme:

1 There should be a dovetail for every 25–30mm (1–1¼in) of material.
2 The space between the dovetails (the narrowest part of the pins) should be approximately 5mm ($\frac{3}{16}$in) in hardwood and 9mm ($\frac{3}{8}$in) in softwood.
3 The slope of the dovetail sides should be approximately 1 in 8 for hardwoods (about 7°) and 1 in 6 for softwoods (about 10°). A steeper angle is required in softwood to achieve the necessary strength.

To demonstrate how the measurement scheme can be worked out, assume that an open-topped box is to be made with hardwood sides 155mm (6⅛in) high. If one dovetail is necessary for every 25–30mm (1–1¼in) of material, the box will have 5 or 6 dovetails at each corner. Assuming that there are to be 6 dovetails then there will be 7 pin spaces, each of 5mm ($\frac{3}{16}$in), and so 35mm (1⅜in) of the material width will be taken up with these. By subtraction there is 120mm (4¾in) of material left for the 6 dovetails and therefore each will be 20mm (approximately ¾in) at its widest point. This example is arranged to work out exactly, but using the general rules as a guide a scheme can be worked out to suit any situation.

The dovetail is shown in its simplest form by the common or through dovetail joint. The marking out for this joint is fairly complex but is explained here in detail. Firstly, shoulder lines are marked all the way around the ends of the pieces to be joined, with a pencil, at a distance of the thickness of the material plus 2mm ($\frac{3}{32}$in) from the end. This extra material will allow the joint to be planed flush after assembly and should be included when cutting the material to length. The dovetail measurements are then squared across the end of the piece which is to have the dovetails, with a knife; the dovetails are usually on the longer sides of box constructions and on the upright sides of cabinets. For the example given these measurements would be 5, 20, 5, 20, 5, 20, 5, 20, 5,

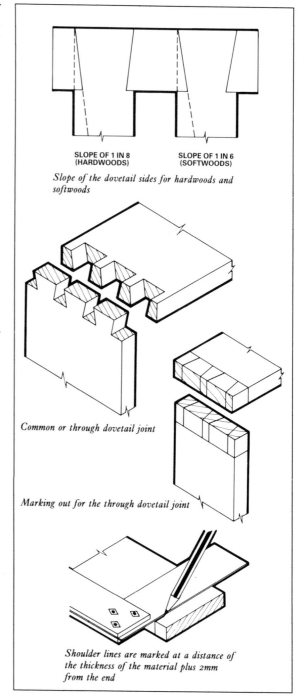

SLOPE OF 1 IN 8 (HARDWOODS)   SLOPE OF 1 IN 6 (SOFTWOODS)

Slope of the dovetail sides for hardwoods and softwoods

Common or through dovetail joint

Marking out for the through dovetail joint

Shoulder lines are marked at a distance of the thickness of the material plus 2mm from the end

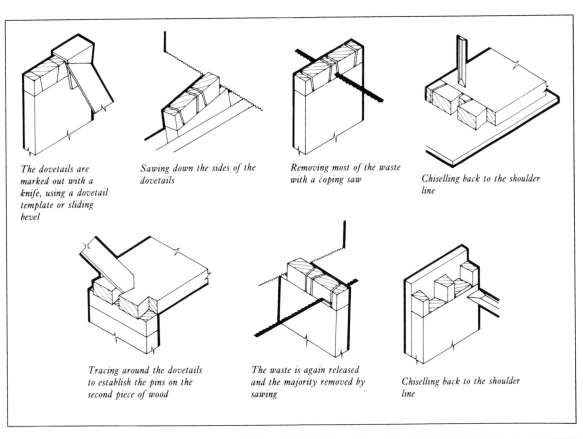

The dovetails are marked out with a knife, using a dovetail template or sliding bevel

Sawing down the sides of the dovetails

Removing most of the waste with a coping saw

Chiselling back to the shoulder line

Tracing around the dovetails to establish the pins on the second piece of wood

The waste is again released and the majority removed by sawing

Chiselling back to the shoulder line

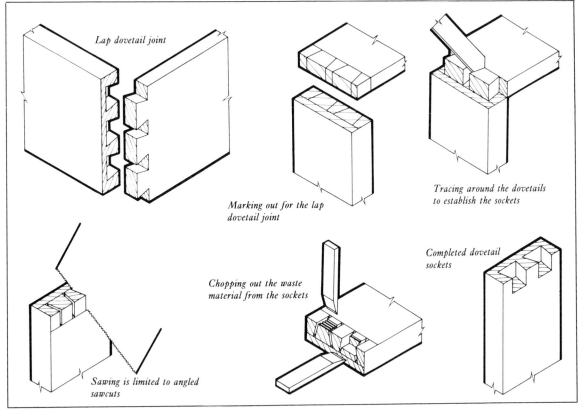

Lap dovetail joint

Marking out for the lap dovetail joint

Tracing around the dovetails to establish the sockets

Completed dovetail sockets

Chopping out the waste material from the sockets

Sawing is limited to angled sawcuts

20 and 5mm (about $\frac{3}{16}$in and $\frac{3}{4}$in respectively). The shapes of the dovetails are then marked down to the shoulder lines on both sides with a knife using a dovetail template or sliding bevel, adjusted to the correct angle. At this stage the shoulder line should be knifed in those positions where it is to be cut. The waste between the dovetails is released by sawing to the waste side of the lines with a back saw, the timber being held in the vice. This operation can be simplified by setting the timber at an angle in the vice so that the sawcuts can be made vertically. A coping saw is used to remove the majority of the waste, the remainder being removed by chiselling back to the shoulder line, working down onto a piece of scrapwood. The waste from the outer pin spaces is simply removed by sawing down the shoulder line. The completed dovetails themselves are used to mark out the sockets into which they will fit. The second piece of timber is placed in the vice and the cut dovetails carefully positioned on top. A knife is used to trace around the dovetails, and if it is found that the lines do not show very clearly the end of the wood can be chalked first. Where these knife lines come to the edges further knife lines are squared down to the shoulder lines on both sides. The waste is again released by sawing and mostly removed with a coping saw, leaving a small amount to be removed with a chisel. This chiselling is most easily carried out in the vice, working horizontally against scrapwood backing. Ideally, the joint will fit straight from the saw but careful trimming may well be necessary to achieve a fit.

The lap dovetail is commonly used for the joint between a drawer front and side, the advantage being that it is only visible from one side. In such situations, the lap dovetail often joins material of different thicknesses. The marking out of the joint varies slightly from that of the common dovetail joint and must incorporate a lap of at least 3mm ($\frac{1}{8}$in), the length of the dovetails being calculated accordingly. The dovetails themselves are cut by the same method as that previously described, and the dovetail sockets are marked out by tracing around them with a knife. The sawing that can be done is limited to angled sawcuts and a chisel and mallet have to be used to chop out the waste material. The chisel is used to alternately segment the waste across the grain and clear the waste with the grain until the sockets are completely opened out.

Adaptations have to be made to the dovetail joint to incorporate grooves and rebates which are common features in box construction for the fitting of tops and bases. To accommodate a rebate a corner should be left in, on one piece, of a length and width which will block off the rebate in the second piece. If a groove is required it should be positioned to pass down the centre of a dovetail and the dovetail then cut away to the depth of the groove. The depth of the socket into which this reduced dovetail will fit must obviously be altered accordingly. To give a neater appearance on the top edge of a box a mitre can be included into the joint and, indeed, such a mitre can be an alternative method of incorporating a rebate.

A further elaboration of the dovetail is the double lapped joint which, when assembled, completely hides the dovetails and has the appearance of a simple lap or rebate joint. The double lapped joint is extremely strong but it is time-consuming to make.

Due to the large glueing areas inside the joints and the tapered dovetail shape itself, the joints are very strong and worth the effort required in their making.

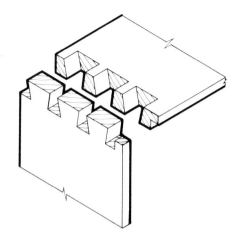

Dovetail adapted to accommodate a rebate

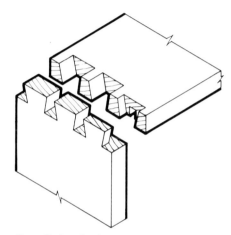

Dovetail adapted to incorporate a groove

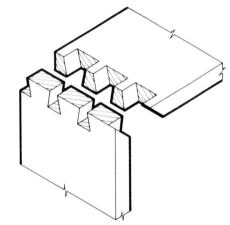

A mitred section on the top edge gives a neater appearance and can also accommodate a rebate

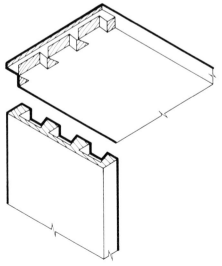

Double lapped dovetail joint

37

9 Widening and lengthening joints

A major advantage of manufactured board materials is that they are available in large board sizes and consequently items such as table tops and cabinet sides can be made in one piece. If solid timber is to be used for a construction which involves a large area it is most likely that narrower boards will have to be joined edge to edge. Unless quarter sawn timber is being used wide boards should be avoided, as in the event of the timber warping the effect will be considerably exaggerated. The narrower the boards the less effect warping will have on the overall flatness of the surface. When joining solid timber boards edge to edge, it is worth spending some time in arranging the boards to achieve the best possible matching of the grain. At the same time it is advisable to alternate the heart sides of the boards so that any timber movement will tend to cancel itself out from one board to the next. Once the arrangement of the boards has been decided the joints should be marked to aid the marking out of any joints and assembly.

A common edge joint is the rubbed butt joint which requires no other preparation than to plane the edges to be joined straight and square. To assemble the joint glue is applied to both surfaces and then the boards are rubbed longitudinally against one another to drive out any surplus glue. Sash cramps are often used to hold the boards in position while the glue sets, but it is sometimes sufficient to place the boards across battens leaning against the wall; the surface tension of the glue and the weight of the top board being enough to hold the joint together.

The tongue and groove joint is commonly used for joining boards together for wall panelling, floor laying and the construction of garden sheds and garage doors. The joint is strong and is both weatherproof and draughtproof. The tongue and groove can be cut with a plough plane using a pair of matching cutters (see Ch. 10) and if desired a feature can be made of the joint by chamfering the top edges of the boards so that a V-shaped channel is formed along the joint. This channel will also serve to disguise any gaps which may result from timber movement. Weatherboarding is timber which has been machined to a section which conveniently edge joints for exterior applications, such as timber cladding on buildings, fencing or garden structures.

The loose tongue and groove joint is easier to cut by hand but it is based on the same principles as the fixed

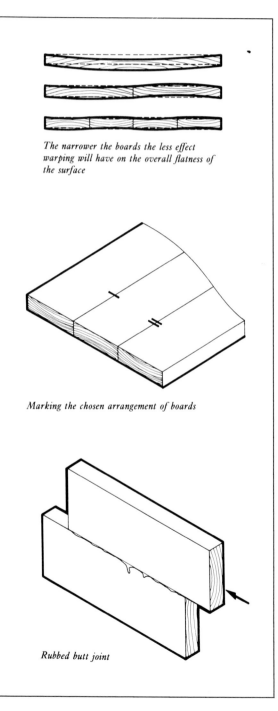

The narrower the boards the less effect warping will have on the overall flatness of the surface

Marking the chosen arrangement of boards

Rubbed butt joint

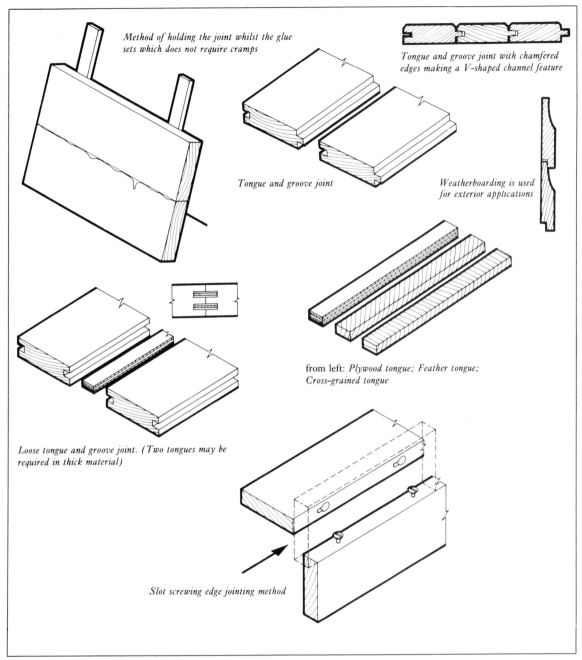

Method of holding the joint whilst the glue sets which does not require cramps

Tongue and groove joint with chamfered edges making a V-shaped channel feature

Tongue and groove joint

Weatherboarding is used for exterior applications

from left: *Plywood tongue; Feather tongue; Cross-grained tongue*

Loose tongue and groove joint. (Two tongues may be required in thick material)

Slot screwing edge jointing method

tongue and groove. The edges to be joined must be planed straight and square and are then ploughed with a groove to match the tongue which is to be fitted. The simplest method of making the loose tongue is to cut a strip of plywood to a width which is slightly less than the total depth of the two grooves. If the tongue is to be made of hardwood the grain must run across the width to achieve strength in the joint. It will be appreciated that such a strip will break very easily whilst being handled and a compromise can be reached by cutting the strip in such a way that the grain runs across the width obliquely. The feather tongue is a compromise

between the strength required in the joint and the ease of cutting and handling of the tongue.

As a general guide the thickness of the tongue should be approximately one-third of the thickness of the material being joined, but on thicker material consideration should be given to the possibility of fitting two tongues.

The slot screwing method of edge jointing requires careful preparation but has the advantage of not needing cramps when being assembled. Without glue the joint can be assembled and taken apart many times, and in this form is a useful temporary fixing. To prepare the

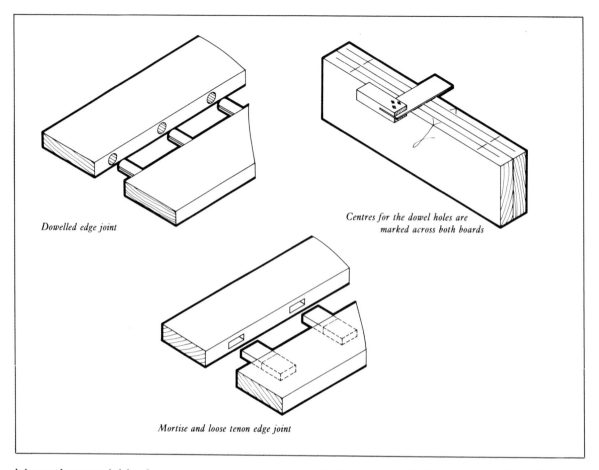

Dowelled edge joint

*Centres for the dowel holes are
marked across both boards*

Mortise and loose tenon edge joint

joint steel countersink head screws are set at appropriate intervals on one board edge along a centre line. In the same positions on the second board, holes are drilled of a size and depth to accept the screw heads. To one side of these holes a second hole is drilled of a diameter equal to the shank of the screw, and the space between each pair of holes is chiselled out to form a keyhole slot. When the boards are assembled the top board is driven along with a mallet which forces the screw heads to bite into the timber, their shape causing the boards to be pulled tightly together. Once the joint has been prepared and tested dry, the screws should be tightened by half a turn before glueing up for permanent assembly.

Dowels are commonly used for edge jointing, both in solid timber and manufactured board constructions. The joint is prepared simply by drilling holes at intervals along gauged centre lines on the board edges to be joined. It is essential that the holes be accurately positioned, and to help in this the centres can be marked by squaring across both boards whilst they are held together. The dowels which are used to hold the boards together should be cut to a length which is 2–3mm (about $\frac{1}{8}$in) shorter than the total depth of the holes into which they fit, and each dowel should have a groove cut along its length and have chamfered ends. (Full details of dowel jointing are given in Ch. 3.)

A further method of edge jointing is achieved by cutting mortises into the edges of the boards into which loose tenons are fitted. To prepare this extremely strong joint the mortises should be cut to a width which is approximately a third of the thickness of the timber and the grain should run along the length of the tenons.

When boards have been edge-jointed together to make a table top or cupboard door it may be advisable to fit battens on the back to hold the construction flat. The fixing of such battens, however, must allow for the movement across the width of the timber which may well occur. This movement is normally allowed for by setting the screws which secure the batten into slots, either side of a static central screw. Countersink head screws may be used in chamfered slots or roundhead screws may be counterbored below the surface. If roundhead screws are to be used it is advisable to fit a washer under the head to facilitate movement.

If battens cannot be used or if it is important to hide the end grain of the edge-jointed construction, wooden clamps can be fitted. A simple and effective method of fitting the clamps is to use a tongue and groove joint, and it is a matter of choice whether the tongue is fixed or loose.

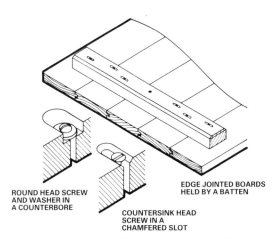

ROUND HEAD SCREW
AND WASHER IN
A COUNTERBORE

COUNTERSINK HEAD
SCREW IN A
CHAMFERED SLOT

EDGE JOINTED BOARDS
HELD BY A BATTEN

Supporting battens may be fitted with screws mounted in slots, to allow for timber movement

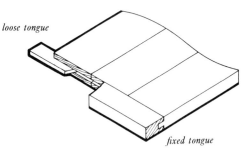

loose tongue

fixed tongue

Wooden clamps may be fitted to support an edge-jointed construction

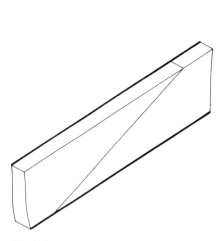

Scarf joint

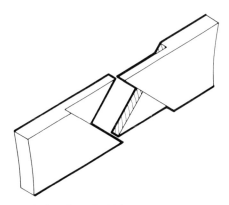

Halved scarf or spliced joint

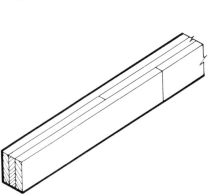

Laminated section with staggered butted end joints

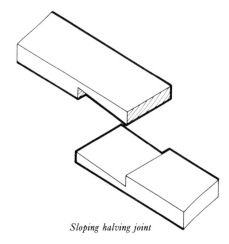

Sloping halving joint

It is sometimes necessary to join pieces of timber end to end to achieve a longer length and there are a number of joints which might be used. The simplest of these joints is the scarf joint which is made by sawing the ends of the pieces to be joined to an angle of approximately 1 in 12, and glueing them together. The halved scarf joint is a more complex joint to prepare but would provide a stronger bond between the two members.

If the section of timber required is being made up by laminating a number of pieces together then lengthening presents no problem. As long as the butted end joints are staggered throughout the lamination there should be no appreciable loss of strength. A lengthening joint which might be more appropriate to cabinet work rather than construction work is the sloping halving joint. The joint is cut in the same way as the more normal parallel-sided halving but the slope which has been introduced into the joint allows it to resist a greater load.

10 Grooves and rebates

The plough plane is supplied with a range of cutters which are suitable sizes to cut grooves for the fitting of standard thicknesses of panel and to help in the cutting of joints. Very often the exact dimensions of a joint will depend on the width of a particular cutter, but if an irregular width of groove is absolutely necessary any size can be cut by making two adjacent grooves with a narrower cutter. The plough plane has a fence which controls the distance of the groove from the edge of the material and also a depth gauge, which will stop the cutting action when the correct depth has been reached.

The rebate plane has a fence which is adjusted to give the required width of rebate and a depth gauge to control the depth. With both of these planes the cut should be started at the far end of the workpiece and, as the groove or rebate progresses, so the start of the cutting stroke is brought further back. In this way any danger of the wood splitting ahead of the blade will be eliminated. With both planes it is also important to apply pressure sideways whilst planing, to keep the fence hard against the edge of the wood.

When grooving or rebating into the edge of a piece of timber it is usually possible to hold the timber in the bench vice. When a groove is being cut into the side of a wide board, or a wide rebate is being cut, there may be problems in holding the work securely. A further situation which may cause problems is the cutting of a groove or rebate into a narrow section of timber; a possible solution here is to cut the groove or rebate into a wide board first and then separate the section required by sawing it from the board. Wider material may be nailed to a thick board held in the vice, the nails being driven through waste material if possible. An alternative is to cramp the material in a sash cramp which in turn is held in the bench vice. It may be possible in some cases to secure the timber onto the bench top with G-cramps, scrapwood being placed between the cramps and the workpiece to prevent damage.

A common edge joint, which is referred to in Ch. 9, is the tongue and groove joint. If a pair of matching cutters is available this joint may be cut with a plough plane. It

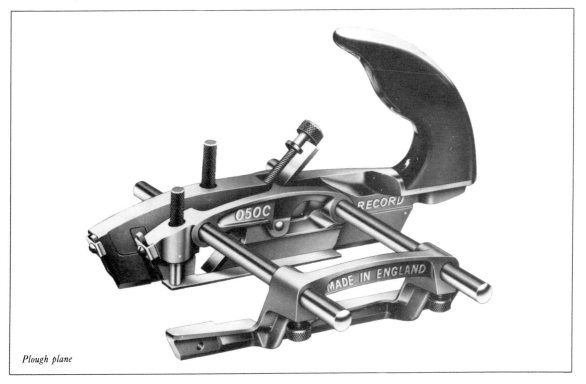

Plough plane

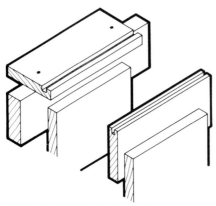

*Holding timber in the vice for grooving.
Wide material left may be nailed to a
board held in the vice*

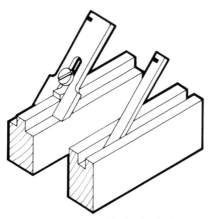

*Matching cutters mounted in the plough plane are
used to cut a tongue and groove joint*

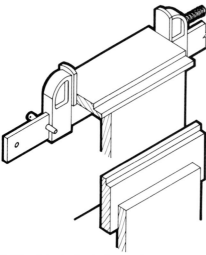

*Holding timber in the vice for grooving.
Wide material left may be nailed to a
board held in the vice*

Rebate plane

will be noted from the diagram that the cutter which forms the tongue has an adjustable depth stop fitted to it.

A groove which runs across the grain is more often referred to as a trench or housing, and the router plane can be extremely useful in levelling the base of a long housing. The router has cutters of different widths and these can be set to cut at a certain depth. It must be appreciated that the waste material must be firstly released by sawing down the sides of the housing before the router is used.

Router plane

11 Joints for manufactured boards

The more traditional woodworking joints are not suitable, or appropriate, to the joining of modern manufactured board materials such as blockboard, plywood or chipboard. There is a large range of knock-down joints and fittings which are specifically designed for use with these board materials, and they are covered in Ch. 12. Dealt with here are those joints which can be used to join manufactured board materials to themselves, or with solid timber, when the method of fixing is just woodwork glue and, possibly, pins.

Cabinet constructions often consist of square-sectioned solid wood corner pieces or legs, joined by plywood panels of a thickness to give sufficient strength. The plywood may be plain if the surface is to be painted, or it may have a veneered surface to give a more decorative exterior appearance. If the plywood panels are thin they can be fitted into rebates cut into the two outward facing sides of the corner piece to give a flush joint. The width of the rebate should be approximately twice the thickness of the plywood. The joint is secured by glueing and pinning and, because the mating line between the two materials is visible, great care must be taken to plane the edge of the plywood panel straight and square. If it is not necessary for the joint to be flush, the thin plywood panels can be fitted into grooves cut into the solid wood corner piece. With this jointing method the outer edge of the corner piece can be rounded or chamfered by planing if desired.

If a thicker plywood panel is necessary, a version of the tongue and groove joint can be used. The plywood panel, which would probably be 12–16mm ($\frac{1}{2}$–$\frac{5}{8}$in) thick, is itself rebated to leave a tongue of at least 6mm ($\frac{1}{4}$in) in width. The solid wood corner piece has grooves ploughed into it so that when the panels are fitted they lie flush with the outer surfaces of the corner piece. If a flush joint is not imperative the grooves can be positioned so that the panels are slightly inset from the faces of the solid wood corner by 3mm ($\frac{1}{8}$in) or so. This inset, or step, will accommodate any slight errors in the positioning of the grooves. Again, the sharpness of the outer corner may be removed by planing.

With even thicker plywood a full tongue and groove joint can be made, with the thickness of the tongue at approximately one-third of the thickness of the plywood. The exact thickness of the tongue will most probably be decided by the width of the cutter which will be used to cut the grooves. The tongue may be cut

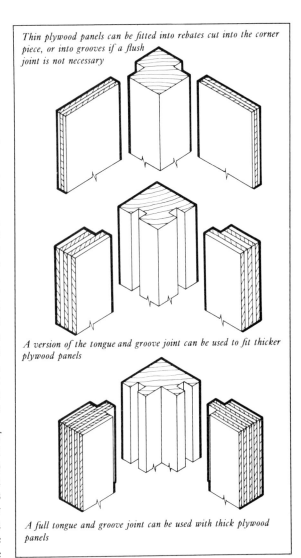

Thin plywood panels can be fitted into rebates cut into the corner piece, or into grooves if a flush joint is not necessary

A version of the tongue and groove joint can be used to fit thicker plywood panels

A full tongue and groove joint can be used with thick plywood panels

with a special blade which is fitted to a plough plane, (see Ch. 10) or the shoulders may be cut separately with a rebate plane. Once again the outer corner may be shaped by planing and with this joint, which has great strength, the inside corner of the solid wood may be rebated out to be flush with the inner surfaces of the plywood panels. This will reduce the amount of intrusion into the internal space of the construction.

The joint chosen to join manufactured board components together at a flush corner will depend on the material being used. Due to the difficulty of cutting rebates in chipboard, either by hand or machine, it is often butt jointed at a corner, and secured by glueing and pinning. If veneered or melamine-faced chipboard is being used the exposed chipboard edge can be covered with iron-on edging strip, before jointing. With the aid of machinery, in the form of a circular saw with a blade which will tilt to 45°, a much neater mitred joint can be considered. This may be supported by an internal corner block glued inside the joint. If it is not seen the corner block would be left square, but it can be planed to a more unobtrusive shape if visible.

The construction of thicker plywoods and block-board suggest the use of the lap or rebate joint for flush corners. With plywood the rebate is cut so as to leave at least two layers to make the overlap of the joint. The rebate may be cut by hand or machine and the joint will only require glueing to secure it. With blockboard the same joint can be used to make a very neat corner by taking the rebate to a depth where only the exterior veneer(s) remain to make the overlap. When this joint is assembled the rather unsightly core strips will be completely hidden.

The mitred corner joint with a loose tongue is a joint which relies on the use of machinery to cut accurately the mitre and the grooves which accept the plywood tongue. The joint is, however, extremely strong and is appropriate for all manufactured board materials of some thickness.

It will be appreciated that the joints described have been developed with the aim of trying to hide unsightly edges of manufactured boards. Due to the advantages of board sizes and the stability of these materials, it is now common practice to use manufactured board materials for tops and table surfaces and methods of edging are required. Iron-on edging strip is generally available in a variety of wood grain patterns, colours and widths and their use is certainly the simplest method of edging. There are, however, circumstances where perhaps a more attractive, robust, or heat- and moisture-proof solution is required and a number of methods are illustrated. Veneered chipboard can be neatly edged with strips of a matching timber. The strips are cut slightly too wide and glued on, an opposite pair at a time. Sash cramps and scrapwood strips are used to hold the lipping in place whilst the glue sets, and then the lipping is carefully planed flush with the board surfaces. The joints at the corners can be mitred or simply lapped. (A lapped joint looks more acceptable if the corner is slightly rounded.)

The other edging methods illustrated are:

Hardwood lipping on plain chipboard with overlapping top veneer.
Deep hardwood lipping strip with overlapping veneer.
Tongued edging strip fitting into grooved board.
Grooved lipping fitted to grooved board with loose plywood tongue.
Laminate edging strip and overlapping laminate top.*
Laminate top surface flush with board and edged with plastic or aluminium edging strip fitted into saw-cut around board.
Clip-on plastic edging strip.
Single lip plastic edging strip.

*The plastic laminate trimmer shown incorporates a number of desirable features. The tool will trim laminates back to the table or worktop edge to which it is being fitted, whether the edge is straight or curved, and in doing so will leave a neat chamfered edge. The tool can also be set to cut narrow edging strips.

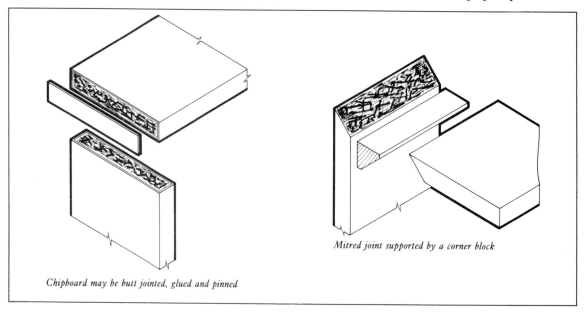

Chipboard may be butt jointed, glued and pinned

Mitred joint supported by a corner block

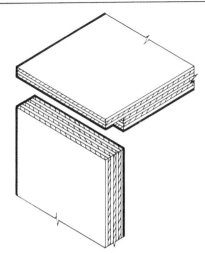

Lap or rebate joint used to achieve a flush corner with thick plywood

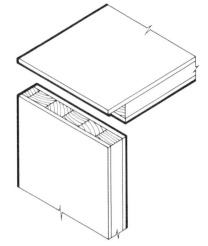

Lap or rebate joint used with blockboard

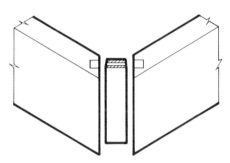

Mitred corner joint with a loose tongue

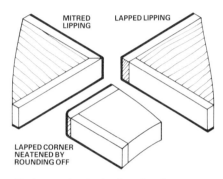

MITRED LIPPING   LAPPED LIPPING

LAPPED CORNER NEATENED BY ROUNDING OFF

Lipping may be mitred or lapped at the corners

HARDWOOD LIPPING WITH OVERLAPPING TOP VENEER

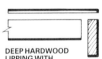

DEEP HARDWOOD LIPPING WITH OVERLAPPING TOP VENEER

CLIP-ON PLASTIC EDGING STRIP

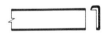

SINGLE LIP EDGING STRIP

TONGUED EDGING STRIP

GROOVED EDGING STRIP FITTED WITH A LOOSE TONGUE

LAMINATE EDGING STRIP WITH OVERLAPPING LAMINATE TOP

LAMINATE TOP WITH PLASTIC OR ALUMINIUM EDGING STRIP

Plastic laminate edge trimmer

12 Knock-down joints and fittings

There is a wide variety of knock-down (K.D.) fittings available on the market and an attempt has been made in this section to select those that are most useful. Knock-down fittings are of particular benefit to the handyman as they allow speedy and accurate construction without the need for complex joinery. Also, their main use is to join the various types of manufactured board, in particular veneered or melamine-faced chipboard, for which the more traditional jointing methods are inappropriate. Most of the fittings only require drilling or screwing, or both, to achieve a joint, although the accurate location of drilling centres and pilot holes is essential for a successful joint.

The most common K.D. corner joint is the two-part plastic corner block. The fitting consists of two plastic blocks which fit together; the moulded lugs on the upper block fit into the counterbored screw holes in the lower block. The two plastic blocks are fastened to the material with No.6 16mm ($\frac{5}{8}$in) countersink head wood screws or chipboard screws. A machine screw holds the blocks firmly together by screwing into the hexagonal nut which is set into the base of the lower block. The corner blocks are available in white or brown and are suitable for making right-angled joints between two panels quickly and effectively. A disadvantage is that the blocks are fairly prominent and are not visually attractive if they are to be seen. A corner block which goes some way in solving this problem is the slimmer and neater assembly block produced by Plasplugs, which is available in white or brown. These two corner joints are easily demountable and this may be an important requirement of the job in hand, but if it is not an essential factor there are other plastic fittings which will make right-angled joints without being so intrusive. The Plasplugs rigid joint is simply screwed into place with No.6 18mm ($\frac{3}{4}$in) countersink head screws and neatly finished by fitting a plastic cover. An alternative fitting is the all-purpose Contijoin which is supplied in a continuous strip of eight fittings. These can be cut off for use either as single units or in pairs, and once they have been screwed in place with No.6 18mm ($\frac{3}{4}$in) screws the flap is closed to cover the unit. Both of these fittings are also available in white or brown. To fit a manufactured board table top to an underframe, or to fix a worktop, the more basic plastic modesty block would probably be used, as in such a situation it would be hidden from view.

The Confirmat connector is a large buttress threaded screw which can be used to join manufactured board materials or solid wood, or a combination of both, in framework or panel constructions. To fit the connectors 7mm ($\frac{5}{16}$in) holes are drilled through the outer panel at appropriate intervals and 5.4mm (about $\frac{3}{16}$in) pilot holes are drilled into the edge of the second panel to a depth of 50mm (2in). The connector screw has a shallow countersink head and if hardwood or melamine-faced materials are being used the outer panel should be lightly countersunk to accept this. On softwoods or veneered chipboard, however, the connector is able to form its own countersink. Plastic caps which push into the pozidriv head of the screws are available in white or brown and a 10mm ($\frac{3}{8}$in) hole drilled to a depth of 2mm ($\frac{3}{32}$in) is required to accommodate them.

The Titus K.D. fitting is particularly strong and has the advantage of hardly intruding into the internal space of the cupboard, and with the use of brown or white cover caps is extremely neat in appearance. The cylindrical bush is fitted into a 25mm (1in) hole which is drilled to a depth of 10mm ($\frac{3}{8}$in), at a centre of 12mm ($\frac{1}{2}$in) from the panel edge. A 10mm ($\frac{3}{8}$in) hole drilled to a depth of 10mm ($\frac{3}{8}$in) into the second panel will take the insert into which the screw which pulls the joint together is driven. The position of the centre of this hole from the panel edge is calculated by subtracting 6mm ($\frac{1}{4}$in) from the thickness of the material being used. Once the insert has been driven home the two parts of the joint will mate together and hold while the screw is screwed home to fix the joint.

The Cam-action fitting is perhaps one of the easiest of all fittings to assemble and take apart again, although the preparation of the panels to fit the device is rather complex. A 25mm (1in) hole is drilled to a depth of 9mm ($\frac{3}{8}$in) in one panel at a centre of 30mm ($1\frac{1}{4}$in) from the panel edge. An 8mm ($\frac{5}{16}$in) hole is then drilled into the edge of the same panel so that it joins the 25mm (1in) hole centrally. On the second panel an 8mm ($\frac{5}{16}$in) hole is drilled to a depth of 8mm ($\frac{5}{16}$in) to accept a plastic bush, into which the special bolt is screwed. As the panels are positioned the head of the bolt locates into the cam cylinder and as the cylinder is turned with a screwdriver the joint is progressively tightened. Cover caps are available in white or brown to render the fitting as unobtrusive as possible.

The dowel fitting is available in two forms, enabling

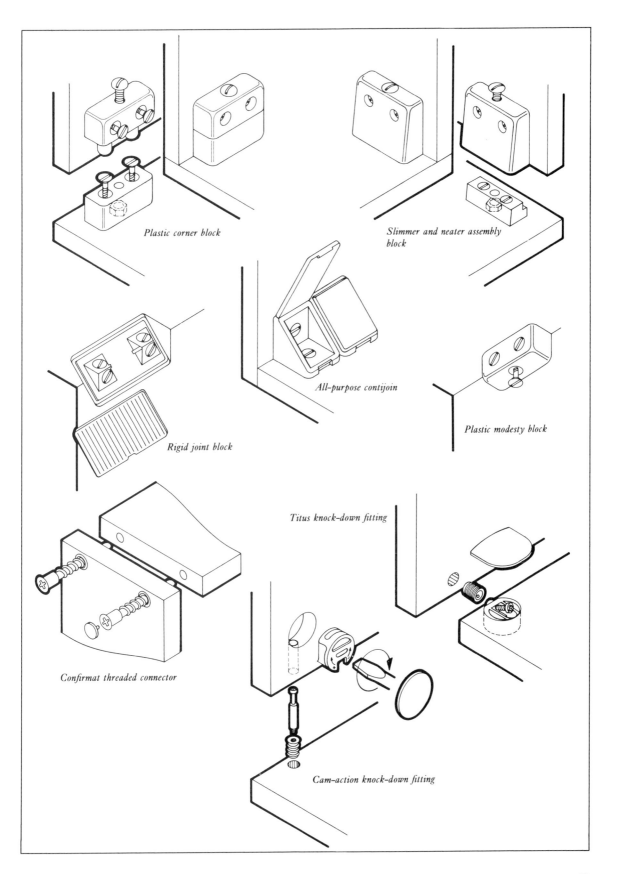

Plastic corner block

Slimmer and neater assembly block

All-purpose contijoin

Rigid joint block

Plastic modesty block

Titus knock-down fitting

Confirmat threaded connector

Cam-action knock-down fitting

the construction of right-angled corner joints as well as the joining of adjacent cabinets with a common centre panel; a useful method of saving material. The fittings are easily mounted into 10mm ($\frac{3}{8}$in) holes drilled into the panels, and although they are not flush their appearance is quite discreet. The main plastic housing of the corner connector is fitted into a hole drilled in the inner panel at a centre of 16mm ($\frac{5}{8}$in) from the edge. The hole in the outer panel, into which the threaded bush is a push fit, is drilled at a centre which is the board thickness plus 6mm ($\frac{1}{4}$in) from the edge; both holes are drilled to a depth of 11mm ($\frac{1}{2}$in). An M6 machine screw is used to tighten the joint. The centre panel connector has a threaded metal dowel which accepts the two machine screws from the plastic housings, positioned on either side of the central panel. The housings are again fitted into 10mm ($\frac{3}{8}$in) holes which in this case are drilled at a centre of 14mm ($\frac{9}{16}$in) from the panel edge. The metal dowel itself is a push fit through a 10mm ($\frac{3}{8}$in) hole in the central panel at a centre which is the board thickness plus 7mm ($\frac{5}{16}$in) from the edge. These connectors are suitable for manufactured board materials of 15–19mm ($\frac{5}{8}-\frac{3}{4}$in) in thickness and have considerable strength.

A fitting which combines the advantages of those K.D. fittings already described is the Cam fitting, which is a recent development and is widely used by furniture manufacturers. The fitting is extremely strong and neat and is available in white, brown or beige to match the material being used. At the time of writing Woodfit is the only known supplier of this fitting to the public but its distribution must become more widespread. The nylon dowel is fitted into an 8mm ($\frac{5}{16}$in) hole drilled centrally into the edge of one panel. This hole should be 25mm (1in) deep to take the dowel and the driving in of the steel pin locks the dowel firmly in place. A 25mm (1in) hole is drilled into the second panel centred at 15.5mm (just under $\frac{5}{8}$in) from the panel edge (for 16mm ($\frac{5}{8}$in) material) to take the cylindrical cam block. When the joint is brought together the cranked dowel end enters the cam which is turned with a screwdriver to lock the joint together.

There are three all-metal K.D. fittings which are useful for frame constructions, e.g. bed frames, and they are all designed so that the load forces the joint more tightly together. The taper connector and the angle fitting are both easily screwed into place and are particularly well suited to large scale work. The flushmount fitting cleverly consists of two identical metal pressings which only take up 3mm ($\frac{1}{8}$in) when assembled. The flushmount is again just screwed into place and has further applications such as the mounting of small cabinets to the wall.

The screw socket is an excellent method of providing a concealed thread in solid timber or chipboard. The socket itself has an external wood thread which allows it to be driven with a screwdriver into an 8mm ($\frac{5}{16}$in) hole drilled to a depth of at least 12mm ($\frac{1}{2}$in). An M6 machine

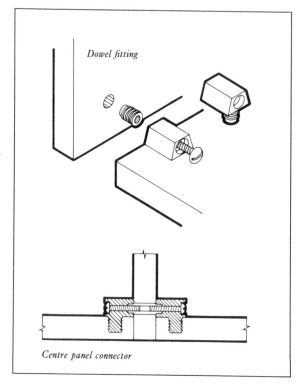

Dowel fitting

Centre panel connector

screw of a suitable length is then used to tighten up the second joint member. A strong joint is achieved with this fitting and it is particularly suitable for large scale work, where the demountable facility is required. A further method of using machine screws for jointing involves the use of a square nut. The nut is fitted into a narrow mortise to a depth which allows the machine screw to be screwed into it to assemble the joint, through a clearance hole. The Scan cross dowel is based on the same principle and is a particularly neat and strong demountable fitting. It is mainly appropriate to solid timber and has wide applications in chair and table construction, for the fitting of rails or rungs, of square or round section, between legs or sides. The cross dowel is a push fit into a 10mm ($\frac{3}{8}$in) hole and has a slot in one end to allow it to be turned to line up with the clearance hole, which must be drilled from the end of the rail to pass through the cross dowel hole. This hole should be 6.5mm ($\frac{1}{4}$in) in diameter to give clearance to the Scan screw which has a countersink head and is turned with a 4mm ($\frac{3}{16}$in) allen key.

A classic method of fitting table legs involves the use of a leg brace plate. A hanger bolt, which has a wood screw thread on one half and a machine thread on the other, is screwed into a pilot hole in the leg, by using the locking action of hexagonal nuts on the machine screw end. The leg brace plate is fitted into saw cuts made across the width of the rails and when the leg is positioned the bolt passes through a hole in the plate. A wing nut is usually used to tighten the joint as it allows for easy dismantling.

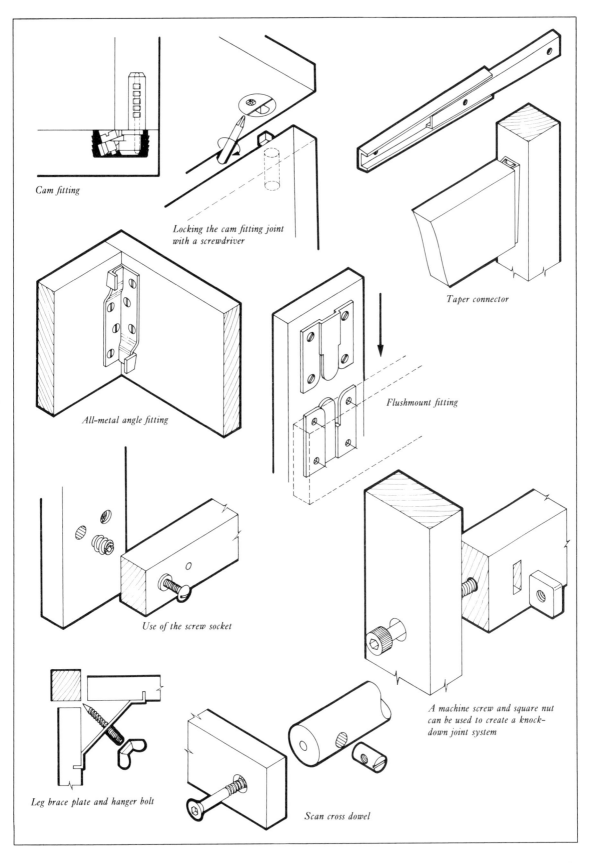

Cam fitting

Locking the cam fitting joint
with a screwdriver

Taper connector

All-metal angle fitting

Flushmount fitting

Use of the screw socket

A machine screw and square nut
can be used to create a knock-
down joint system

Leg brace plate and hanger bolt

Scan cross dowel

13 Nailing and screwing

The various methods of nailing and screwing are dealt with here in some detail as nails and screws are often used instead of, or in addition to, jointing techniques. The more common types of nail and screw are shown below, and their uses outlined. Wherever possible the length of nail or screw to be used should be three times the thickness of the wood being fixed to achieve sufficient grip.

round head screw: often used to fix metal fittings to wood, e.g. hasp and staple, and is frequently black-japanned to suit exterior situations.

raised countersink screw: an attractive looking screw which is used for fixing door furniture and wall fittings. A chromium plated finish is common on these screws.

countersink head screw: the most common screw head shape which is used for all general purposes. They are mainly supplied in plain steel.

twinfast screw: these screws have been developed for use with manufactured boards, in particular chipboard. The screws have twin threads to give greater holding power and these run right up to the head.

coach screw: coach screws have an hexagonal head and are turned with a spanner. The thread is coarse and the screws are used for heavy construction work, e.g. garden benches and sheds.

cut brad nail (25–125mm, 1–5in): this has extremely good holding power and is mainly used to fix floorboards.

round wire nail (25–150mm, 1–6in): the large head on this nail prevents the wood pulling over the head. The nails are mainly used for softwood work where appearance is not important.

oval wire nail (12–100mm, $\frac{1}{2}$–4in): the oval is used for most domestic joinery. The shape of the oval means that it is less likely to split the wood and it can easily be punched below the surface and covered.

round wire lost head: this nail is also used for joinery work. The small head can be easily concealed.

panel pin (12–50mm, $\frac{1}{2}$–2in): the panel pin has many uses including the fixing of beads, panels and joints.

panel pin (deep drive): the deep drive pin is designed to finish below the surface when fixing plywood or hardboard panels, where it will be barely visible.

veneer pin: a thinner version of the panel pin used for finer work.

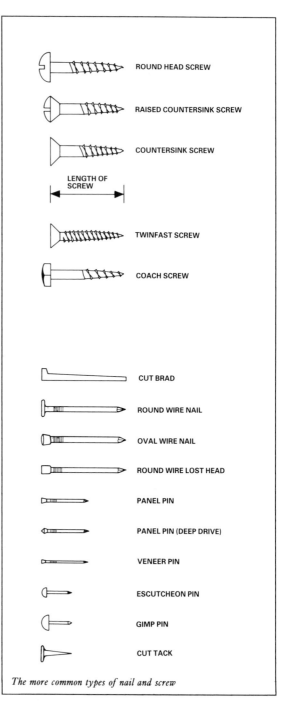

The more common types of nail and screw

escutcheon pin: a short, brass, dome-headed nail which is used to fix metal protective plates in position, e.g. keyhole plate.

gimp pin: gimp pins are used to fix upholstery, the large head holding material without causing it to tear. For a better appearance they are often brass-finished.

cut tack: tacks can be used to fix upholstery underneath a seat platform and in other situations where they will not be seen.

Screws are most commonly made from steel or brass and are sometimes coated to give particular properties, e.g. chromium-plated for appearance and rust-proofing and black-japanned for exterior use. Screw sizes vary in thickness from 0–22 gauge and screw lengths range from 6–150mm ($\frac{1}{4}$–6in). In addition to the traditional slot-headed screw, the Phillips and Pozidriv screw head types are in regular use. These screwheads have the advantage of reducing the chance of the screwdriver slipping and damaging the surrounding work as they locate the screwdriver tip more firmly. They also allow more force to be exerted on the screw. Just three point sizes of Phillips or Pozidriv screwdriver will fit all screw sizes up to gauge 12.

The preparation required before inserting a screw will depend on the type of screw. The traditional round head or countersink head wood screws require two holes to be drilled. The clearance hole is drilled through the piece of wood which is to be fixed and should be equal to the diameter of the shank of the screw; the pilot hole which is drilled into the wood that the screw will grip into should be approximately half of the diameter of the clearance hole. The countersink head screw also requires a countersink to allow the head to lie flush. This is easily achieved with a countersink bit fitted into a drill. Twinfast or chipboard screws require less preparation and all that is needed is the one pilot hole through both pieces of wood. To save time in preparing for normal wood screws a screwsink can be used to make the clearance hole, pilot hole and countersink in one operation.

screw gauge	clearance hole	pilot hole
2	2.2mm	1mm
4	2.8mm	1.4mm
6	3.6mm	1.8mm
8	4.4mm	2.2mm
10	5mm	2.6mm
12	5.8mm	3mm
14	6.4mm	3.2mm

N.B. Estimates of imperial measurements can best be made here by using the conversion: 0.8mm = $\frac{1}{32}$in

If the exact drill size is not available the choice of the nearest, whether smaller or larger, will depend on the material being used. A slightly smaller drill can be used for softwood but for hardwood a slightly larger drill should be chosen to prevent splitting.

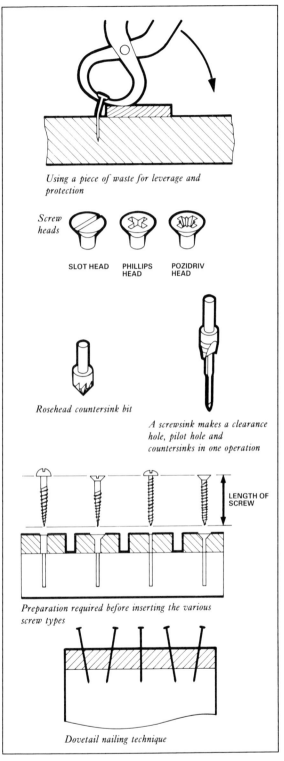

Using a piece of waste for leverage and protection

Screw heads

SLOT HEAD   PHILLIPS HEAD   POZIDRIV HEAD

Rosehead countersink bit

A screwsink makes a clearance hole, pilot hole and countersinks in one operation

LENGTH OF SCREW

Preparation required before inserting the various screw types

Dovetail nailing technique

Some joints are often nailed, in addition to glueing, to further secure the joint, e.g. the butt joint and the lap joint, and a useful technique is dovetail nailing. A central pin or nail is driven in to hold the boards in alignment and pairs of nails are driven in at alternate angles so that the joint is able further to resist being pulled apart. There is always the problem of splitting when driving nails in and to some extent this can be overcome when using large nails by making a pilot hole with a drill or bradawl, but it is the positioning of the nails which is particularly important. There are various arrangements for the staggering of nails to prevent splitting when nailing boards to battens or when nailing the corners of frameworks. The principle behind each of the arrangements is to avoid the nails coinciding in one line along the grain.

If the thickness of the timber does not allow a nail of the correct length to be used, there is the option of bending the nails over on the far side of the joint (clenching) to achieve extra strength. Although clenching is rather unsightly it is an acceptable practice on exterior work. The nails can be simply hammered through and bent over at the back, but there is the danger of being cut or catching clothing on the exposed points. These can be punched below the surface with a large nail set, or a different clenching method can be used whereby the nail, once driven through, is bent into a U shape, with pliers or around a bar, and then is hammered back inside the timber so that the point is hidden.

In cases where comparatively thin board is being screwed into place through a thicker piece, e.g. the fixing of a manufactured board table top to an underframe, there are various techniques to avoid the use of long screws. The alternatives are to counterbore the rail so that the screwhead is able to pass up through into the rail or to make a pocket in the side of the rail from which the screw can be inserted. This pocket may be made either by drilling a large diameter hole into the rail or by making a smaller angled hole.

If nails are to be hidden they can be easily punched below the surface with a nail punch or set, and the head covered over with a suitable coloured stopping. A second method of secret nailing is achieved by lifting a shaving with a gouge and driving the nail in so that it is covered when the shaving is glued back in place.

Screw heads can be hidden or made more visually acceptable by a number of methods. Plastic screw covers are available which consist of an artificial countersink socket through which the screw is driven, the hinged flap being snapped closed to hide the screw. These fittings do protrude however, and a neater job is achieved with screw caps which locate into a counterbore which has to be drilled before the screw is fitted. The appearance of a screw which may need to be withdrawn a number of times can be improved by the use of a screw cup. This also has the effect of increasing the bearing area of the screw head, which may be important in softwood. The mirror screw is very common and consists of a chromed dome which screws into the screw head itself, once the screw has been driven home. As its name suggests, this is used for fixing

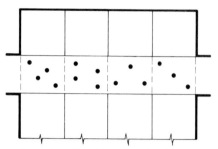

Staggering nail positions for nailing boards to supporting battens

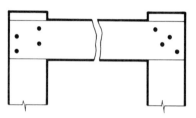

Staggered nail positions for nailing the corners of frameworks

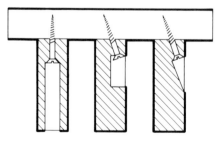

Methods of nail clenching

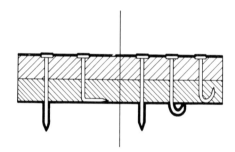

COUNTERBORE   POCKET SCREWING

Counterboring to reduce the length of screw required left and pocket screwing

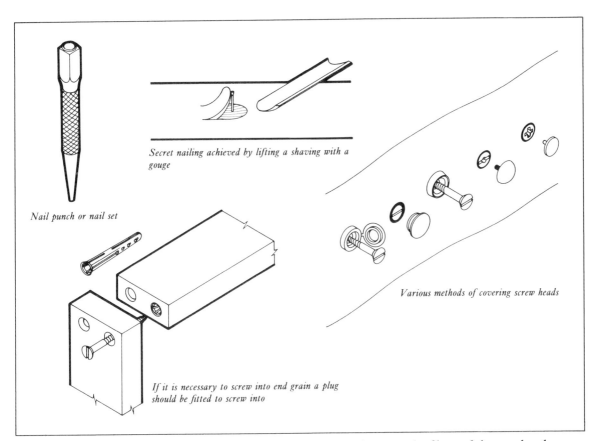

Nail punch or nail set

Secret nailing achieved by lifting a shaving with a gouge

Various methods of covering screw heads

If it is necessary to screw into end grain a plug should be fitted to screw into

sheets of material such as a mirror to timber or to the wall. A further advantage of the Pozidriv type of screw head is that it allows a plastic cover cap to be fitted into the slot. Superdriv screws have this facility and white or brown cover caps are available (shown left to right).

The grip of a screw depends on the threads cutting their way between the fibres of the wood and consequently it is bad practice to attempt to screw into end grain, as little grip can be gained. By fitting a plug into a drilled hole to accept the screw a perfectly strong joint can be achieved.

14 Finishing and finishes

It is at the finishing stage of a job that patience and care must be exercised to ensure that the full potential of a piece is realised. When all the joint cutting is completed there is a temptation to rush ahead and assemble a job, but it is precisely whilst the components are still separate that the groundwork for a good finish should be carried out. All the inside faces should be rubbed down with a medium abrasive to remove pencil marks and scratches, and then rubbed down again with a fine abrasive to leave a smooth and unmarked surface. (It is often more convenient to rub down the *outside* surfaces after assembly, as this may be part of a cleaning-up process which includes planing joints off flush.)

Abrasives are usually supplied in sheets measuring 280 × 230mm (11 × 9in). These can be cut into six and used very economically, wrapped around a cork block when working on flat surfaces. The use of a cork block ensures an even pressure throughout the abrasive and the slight give in the cork lessens the danger of tearing the paper. The principle of abrasives is that successively finer grits will remove the scratches left by the previous grade and leave finer scratches in their place. When the finest abrasive is used the scratches left are so small that they are invisible to the human eye. This is only the case if the abrasive is worked in the direction of the grain, as even the finest will leave marks across the grain. It is however, acceptable to work obliquely across the grain to remove particularly stubborn marks provided that the rubbing down is continued with the grain. When a softwood surface is being prepared for painting, the rubbing down should be carried out obliquely to the grain to prevent a rippled effect being created by the quicker removal of the softer wood from between the annual rings.

There are four abrasive materials available and each is suitable for particular situations. The most common is glasspaper, which consists of glass bonded to a paper backing. Although it has the advantage of being inexpensive, glass is a soft abrasive and soon loses its cutting power, limiting its usefulness to hand sanding. Garnet is a red-coloured mineral which makes a longer lasting abrasive, although it is more expensive. Aluminium oxide is a tough abrasive which is a grey-brown colour and it is this material which is often used on the belts and discs on sanding machinery. These abrasives are available in open coat or close coat forms, the difference being in the amount of abrasive grit that has

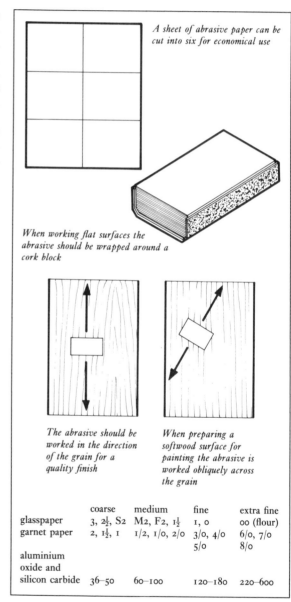

A sheet of abrasive paper can be cut into six for economical use

When working flat surfaces the abrasive should be wrapped around a cork block

The abrasive should be worked in the direction of the grain for a quality finish

When preparing a softwood surface for painting the abrasive is worked obliquely across the grain

	coarse	medium	fine	extra fine
glasspaper	3, 2½, S2	M2, F2, 1½	1, 0	00 (flour)
garnet paper	2, 1½, 1	1/2, 1/0, 2/0	3/0, 4/0 5/0	6/0, 7/0 8/0
aluminium oxide and silicon carbide	36–50	60–100	120–180	220–600

been bonded to the backing material. Open coat sheets are less likely to clog and would be preferable when rubbing down softwoods. Silicon carbide is the abrasive grit which is used to produce wet or dry paper. In its fine grades this is often used to flat a coat of varnish or paint before applying another coat.

If a considerable amount of moulding or shaped section needs to be rubbed down it may be worthwhile preparing a block to wrap the abrasive paper around to achieve accurate sanding, or a length of dowel for the inside of holes and curves.

A useful tool for finishing hardwoods, especially if the grain is interlocked or irregular, is the scraper. The scraper is quite simply a rectangular piece of hardened sheet steel which is sharpened in such a way that a hook is produced along the cutting edge. In use the scraper is bent and inclined forward by pressing on the back with the thumbs and as it is pushed across the material surface small shavings are taken. An alternative to the scraper is to use a piece of glass cut to a convenient size. As the glass cannot be bent in the same way as the steel sheet it should be cut with a slight curve along what is to be the cutting edge. As the edge becomes dull, so a new edge can be produced by re-cutting the glass.

A sharp and finely-set smoothing plane can save a lot of time otherwise spent with abrasive paper and will help to achieve a high quality finish. Apart from the adjustment which can be made to the depth of cut there is a further adjustment which can be made which will improve the surface left by the plane. By moving the frog of the plane forward the effective width of the mouth is reduced and a greater control over the way the shaving is lifted from the wood is achieved.

In bringing a wood surface to the desired level of finish wood stopping may have to be used to fill cracks, joint gaps or indentations. Stopping is available in a wide range of colours to match the more common timbers. Some hardwoods have what is called an open grain, and even when finely sanded the surface will show small indentations or pits. To achieve a completely smooth finish coloured wood filler should be used. The filler is firstly wiped into the surface in a circular motion with a cloth and then rubbed hard across the grain. To remove the surplus a clean cloth is run lightly along the grain; once the filler has dried the surface is sanded.

When a surface has been fully rubbed down there is a choice of finishes which can be applied and the desired appearance, purpose and working conditions of the piece will dictate this choice. If the job is to be dyed, either to deepen the natural colour of the wood or to colour it, the dye should be applied to the bare wood. Solvent-based dyes are recommended and are best applied with a cloth, making quick overlapping strokes over the surface. The dye should be left to dry and wiped over with a clean cloth to remove any surplus before a clear finish is put over the top. (A second coat of dye may have to be applied to achieve the depth of colour required.)

The first step in applying a varnish is to seal the surface of the wood with a sealer, e.g. thinned polyurethane varnish, spirit-based white polish or thinned cellulose lacquer. When dry, the wood should be lightly rubbed down with extra fine abrasive to remove any

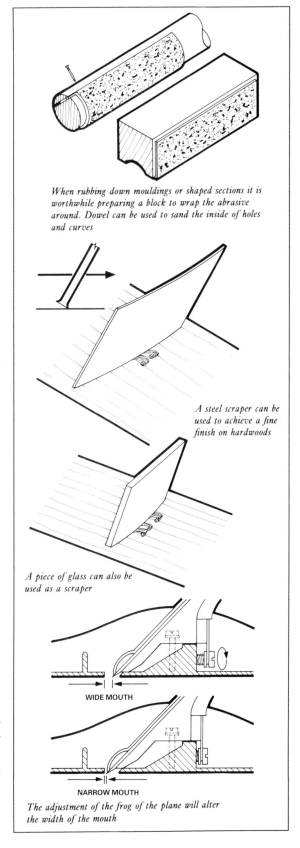

When rubbing down mouldings or shaped sections it is worthwhile preparing a block to wrap the abrasive around. Dowel can be used to sand the inside of holes and curves

A steel scraper can be used to achieve a fine finish on hardwoods

A piece of glass can also be used as a scraper

WIDE MOUTH

NARROW MOUTH

The adjustment of the frog of the plane will alter the width of the mouth

Orbital sanding machine

Belt sanding machine

raised grain. The required number of layers of the chosen finish can then be built up, each layer being left until it is completely dry and lightly rubbed down before the next coat is brushed on.

Two or three coats of white polish will produce an attractive interior finish for furniture and fittings, although it is not very durable. The finishing process is best completed by lightly applying wax polish with the finest grade of steel wool, the wax being allowed to harden and then being polished up with a soft cloth. (Further layers of wax should be applied with a cloth.) If a quality wax is used this will result in a dull glow in the wood which is most attractive. There is no doubt that the best wax to use is beeswax, which can be dissolved in turpentine to make it more workable.

One-pot polyurethane is now in common use and is made by a number of manufacturers in gloss, satin or eggshell and matt forms, for interior or exterior use. These varnishes are a good way of producing a moisture- and heat-resistant surface, although the gloss finish sometimes gives a rather unnatural look. A recommended method of taking advantage of the scratch and knock resistance of polyurethanes but avoiding the rather glassy appearance is to use steel wool and wax over satin or matt polyurethane varnish. Two-pack polyurethane varnish gives an extremely tough and resistant finish which has numerous applications in kitchens, bathrooms and outside the house.

To protect timber which is out of doors there is a number of preservatives which are simply brushed on and allowed to dry. Creosote is most suitable for fencing and garden buildings but colour may be a more important factor on wall cladding or garden furniture. There are brightly coloured wood protection systems which have recently become available which give lasting protection, and because they are translucent they enhance the natural appearance of the timber.

If wood is to be painted the sequence of primer, undercoat and top coat should be followed to ensure adequate protection. Two coats of gloss are recommended for exterior work and particular care should be taken to seal end grain completely. When children's toys or nursery equipment is being painted it is most important to check that the paint is non-toxic, and most coloured enamels and lacquers will conform to this requirement.

Some finishing work can be quickened by the use of sanding machinery, and amongst the many different makes and models on the market there are essentially two different kinds of machine. The orbital sander has a flat rubber base to which either one-third or half of a sheet of abrasive paper is clamped, depending on the model. The mechanism in the machine causes the base to move in a circular motion, thus rubbing down the work as pressure is applied. The model illustrated has a particular advantage in that the orbital motion can be used for heavy sanding, then by moving a lever the movement can be changed to a linear motion for finishing work. Obviously a finer abrasive would be fitted for this finishing work. The belt sander is mainly used for large areas and for heavier sanding operations. Belts of different abrasive grades can be fitted and the machine has an efficient dust collecting system.

RECOMMENDED FINISHING MATERIALS

stopping and wood filler – Brummer (Clam-Brummer Ltd)

wood dyes – Colron (Sterling Roncraft); Sadolin (Sadolin U.K. Ltd)

polyurethane varnish – PU 15 (Furniglas, Evode Ltd); Woodplan (International Paints)

two-pack polyurethane – Woodplan (International Paints)

wax polish – Colron (Sterling Roncraft)

coloured lacquer – Japlac (International Paints)

coloured enamel – Humbrol (Borden U.K. Ltd)

15 Adhesives and assembly

A job should always be cramped up dry before finally assembled with glue, to check that the joints can be brought up tight and also that the overall dimensions of the assembled piece are correct. In carrying out this procedure the cramps will be set to the correct lengths and any scrapwood required to protect the job from damage by the cramps will have been prepared.

When applying glue to a joint, thought should be given to the way it comes together, and the glue should be spread in such a way that assembling pushes the glue into the joint. This means that with mortise and tenon joints most of the glue should be spread around inside the mortise itself, while the holes of a dowel joint should be liberally lined with glue, and in a dovetail joint the glue should mainly be spread around the pins. The overall aim of glueing up is to apply glue to every surface which comes into contact with another, as it is the glueing area within joints which provides the strength.

Unless glue is being used in conjunction with nails or screws, pressure is normally required to hold a job in the correct position while the glue sets. For small scale work the bench vice or G-cramp, or a combination of both, can be used. Work on a larger scale will demand longer cramps and the sash cramp, which is available in various lengths, is the accepted tool to use. Cramp heads are intended for use on jobs which demand a greater length of cramp than can be achieved with sash cramps, even with extension bars fitted. The cramp heads are fitted to battens and, because of their relative cheapness, can perhaps be considered as alternatives to sash cramps. A successful cramping device can be made in the workshop from 47×22mm ($1\frac{7}{8} \times \frac{7}{8}$in) softwood or hardwood and 12mm ($\frac{1}{2}$in) plywood. The mechanism by which the

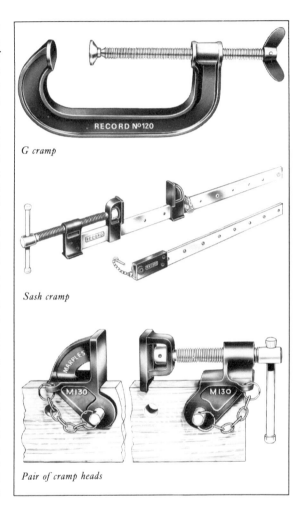

G cramp

Sash cramp

Pair of cramp heads

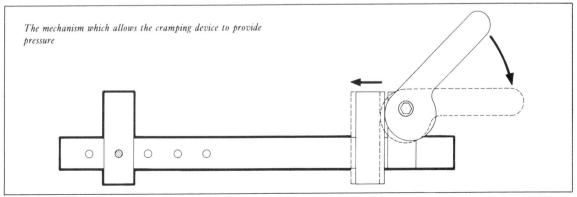

The mechanism which allows the cramping device to provide pressure

cramp works is in the shape of the lever and the fact that it is pivoted off-centre. This acts as a cam, and as the lever is pushed down the cramp head slide is pushed along the batten, up to a total distance of 25mm (1in). The tail slide of the cramp is locked into position with a 12mm (½in) dowel fitted into a hole drilled into the main batten, and rather than drilling holes at regular intervals along the batten and weakening it unnecessarily it is suggested that the holes be drilled in the appropriate places as they become necessary. Full details of the construction of the cramping device are given in the diagram.

When frames are being cramped up it is important to position the cramp down the centre of a member to keep the construction square. If the joint shoulders have been cut correctly a joint should cramp up square; in the event of a try square showing a corner to be out of square, the cramp can be angled slightly to correct the error. When an open-ended frame is being cramped there can be an advantage in cutting a piece of wood to the same length as the distance between shoulders on the rail to maintain the correct dimension at the open end.

In some cases is may be difficult to use a try square to check the corners of a frame or box, or the use of a try square may not be appropriate because the pressure from the cramps has caused the timber to bow slightly. In these cases squareness is checked by comparing the lengths of the diagonals; if they are equal in length the construction must be square. On small scale work a steel rule can be used for this, but for larger work a squaring rod will be needed. A squaring rod consists simply of a thin strip of wood which is sharpened to a point at one end and is used by pushing the point into one corner and marking off on the rod the position of the corner diagonally opposite. The same procedure is carried out across the second diagonal and the cramps adjusted until the marks on the rod coincide. The same procedure can be carried out very accurately with two steel rules held together with the rounded ends pushed into the corners of the frame or box.

There is a second important check which must be made before leaving a frame to dry and that is to check that the frame is flat and not in-winding or twisted. This can be done quite simply by sighting along the length of the frame, correcting any error by adjusting cramps, or by weighting or cramping the frame down onto a surface which is known to be true, e.g. a bench top.

If thin edging material or lipping is being fixed to the edge of a board, a thick scrapwood strip will be needed to distribute the pressure evenly from the cramps along the whole length of the lipping strip. When two or three boards are being cramped edge to edge to make up a large area, cramps should be positioned on both sides to prevent the boards from lifting and possibly springing out of the cramps. A common situation which must be overcome is the cramping of joints which have been deliberately cut to overlap slightly, so that they can be planed flush after assembly. In these cases the scrapwood and cramps can be positioned just inside the joints to allow the overlap. If this in turn causes problems of bowing along the length of the box or frame members, support can be given in the form of thick sections of timber cut to length and positioned inside the construction.

If mitred joints are to be held together to dry, the mitre cramp can be useful. When making picture frames the cramp is usually used to hold each joint in turn while pins are driven in to secure them. The frame clamp is a simple device which allows a complete frame to be glued and assembled in one operation. The length of cord supplied with the clamp is 3.5m (138in) and this allows frames of some considerable size to be handled. The web clamp is an extremely useful device which is supplied with 3.5m (138in) of nylon webbing. The clamp has a ratchet action which is operated with a screwdriver, and considerable pressure can be achieved on all types of work. The particular advantage of the web clamp is that it can be used on round or irregular shaped pieces as well as square frame and box constructions.

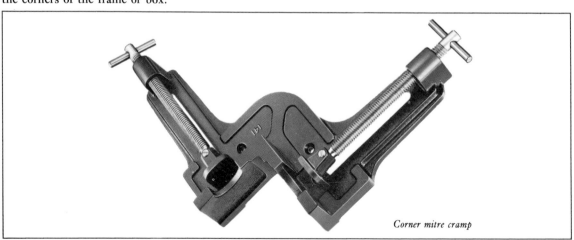

Corner mitre cramp

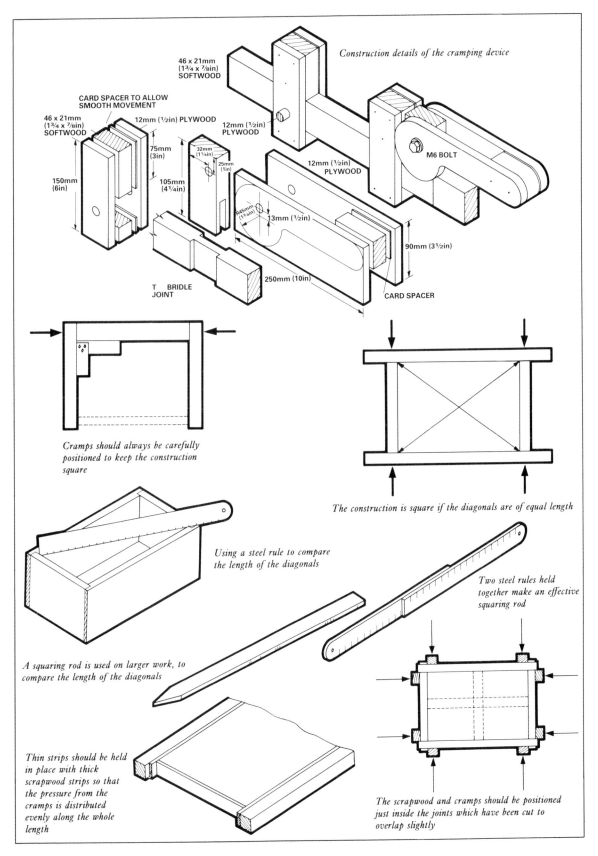

Construction details of the cramping device

46 x 21mm (1¾ x ⅞in) SOFTWOOD

CARD SPACER TO ALLOW SMOOTH MOVEMENT

46 x 21mm (1¾ x ⅞in) SOFTWOOD

12mm (½in) PLYWOOD

12mm (½in) PLYWOOD

12mm (½in) PLYWOOD

M6 BOLT

75mm (3in)

32mm (1¼in)

25mm (1in)

150mm (6in)

105mm (4¼in)

R45mm (1¾in)

13mm (½in)

90mm (3½in)

250mm (10in)

T   BRIDLE
JOINT

CARD SPACER

Cramps should always be carefully positioned to keep the construction square

The construction is square if the diagonals are of equal length

Using a steel rule to compare the length of the diagonals

Two steel rules held together make an effective squaring rod

A squaring rod is used on larger work, to compare the length of the diagonals

Thin strips should be held in place with thick scrapwood strips so that the pressure from the cramps is distributed evenly along the whole length

The scrapwood and cramps should be positioned just inside the joints which have been cut to overlap slightly

Frame clamp

Web clamp

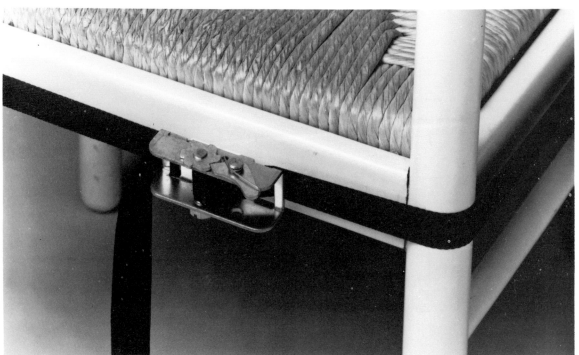

ADHESIVES

adhesive type	uses	brand names	manufacturer
PVA (Polyvinyl Acetate)	All furniture construction – for indoor use	Evo-stik Resin W Dunlop Woodworker	Evode Ltd Dunlop Ltd
Urea-formaldehyde	Moisture resistant and moderately weatherproof. Furniture construction	Cascamite One-shot Aerolite 306	Borden U.K. Ltd Ciba-Geigy plc
Resorcinol-formaldehyde	Completely weatherproof and suitable for exterior work. Furniture and joinery	Aerodux 500	Ciba-Geigy plc
Epoxy resin	Particularly useful for bonding dissimilar materials together, e.g. wood to metal	Araldite UHU Strong Bond	Ciba-Geigy plc Beecham UHU Ltd
Contact adhesive	Plastic laminate to tops and fabric, leather and foam fabrication	Thixofix Evo-stik Impact	Dunlop Ltd Evode Ltd

16 Drills and drilling techniques

Traditionally, there are two types of drill which are used in the workshop, the carpenter's brace and the hand drill. To some extent these have been superseded by the portable electric drill, but there is still some advantage in using the brace and hand drill for some jobs.

The twist drill is mainly used in the hand drill or power drill, most taking diameters up to 8–10mm ($\frac{5}{16}$–$\frac{3}{8}$in). (Twist drills can be used in braces which are fitted with universal jaws.) When drilling small diameter holes there is little risk of splitting-out on the far side, but with most drilling operations it is wise to work against scrapwood as a precaution. Very often it is necessary to be able to gauge the depth of the hole being drilled accurately. If a pillar drill, or a power drill fitted to a drill stand, is being used, the depth can usually be set, but with other types of drill alternative methods are required. A piece of tape wrapped around the drill is a simple but effective way of measuring depth, but it only acts as an indicator rather than an actual stop. To provide a stop a piece of rubber tube or cork can be threaded onto the drill.

Power drill fitted into a drill stand

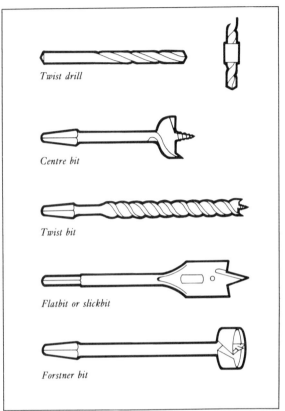

Twist drill

Centre bit

Twist bit

Flatbit or slickbit

Forstner bit

The centre bit and twist bit are turned with a carpenter's brace and each is suited to particular drilling operations. The centre bit is used for boring shallow, large diameter holes. Twist bits, on the other hand, are more suited to the boring of long holes of smaller diameters, e.g. dowel holes. These bits are particularly useful when drilling into end grain.

The flatbit, or slickbit, is exclusively for use in a power drill as it relies on speed to cut cleanly. The long pointed centre on the drill means that blind, or stopped, holes can rarely be cut without the centre breaking through to the far side of the material, but an advantage of the centre is that it will hold the drill on course when drilling at an angle.

The forstner bit usually has a square shank for fitting into the brace, and although it makes rather slow progress through the wood it is particularly useful for blind holes. The bit leaves a flat bottom to the hole and there is little centre marking.

When boring a hole with a bit which has a long centre the possibility of an untidy exit to the hole on the far side, even though scrapwood is used, can be avoided. With the workpiece held in the vice the hole is bored from one side until the point breaks through on the far side. The bit is then withdrawn, the workpiece reversed, and the hole completed from the second side. When drilling horizontally it is not too difficult to hold the drill square to the working surface and the holes will usually be quite accurate, but where the drilling is being carried out vertically more difficulty is often encountered. To provide a drilling guide a try square, or a jig made of scrapwood, can be rested on the working surface to work against.

When stepped holes are being drilled, e.g. when making a counterbore, it is important always to drill the larger diameter first so as not to lose the centre for the second drilling operation. Both with bits and twist drills the centre is clearly established for the drilling of the smaller diameter hole.

The fitting of most modern hinge mechanisms into manufactured board material involves the drilling of large diameter blind holes and end mills are commonly available for this operation. The mills are designed for use in a power drill and make a clean, flat-bottomed hole, and in some cases have a built-in depth stop in the form of a flange at the top of the cutting block.

The plug cutter is again for use in a power drill and is available in a range of sizes which will cut plugs to cover screw heads which have been counterbored.

To drill irregular sizes of hole up to large diameters the expansive bit can be very useful. Fitted into a brace, the larger model can be adjusted to any diameter required from 18 to 75mm ($\frac{3}{4}$–3in). Also useful for the cutting of larger holes is the hole cutter, which usually has seven saw-tooth edged blades which will cut a range of hole sizes up to 65mm ($2\frac{1}{2}$in) in diameter. Although the cutter is designed primarily to cut holes, the waste discs which are produced can often be useful.

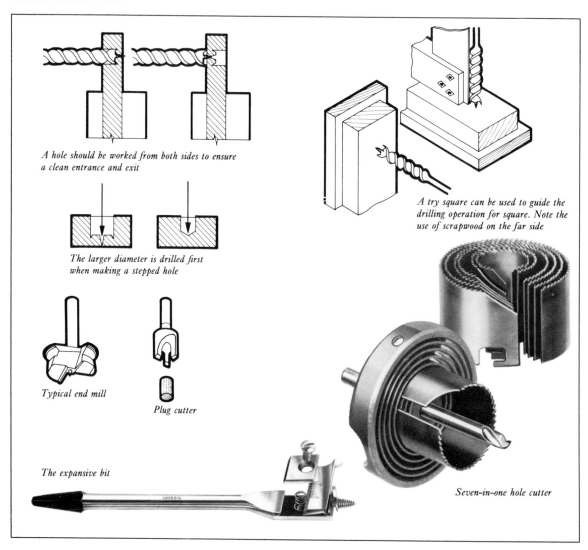

A hole should be worked from both sides to ensure a clean entrance and exit

The larger diameter is drilled first when making a stepped hole

Typical end mill

Plug cutter

The expansive bit

A try square can be used to guide the drilling operation for square. Note the use of scrapwood on the far side

Seven-in-one hole cutter

17 Drawer construction

There are various ways of constructing the basic box which is needed for a drawer. The method chosen will depend on the piece of furniture for which the drawer is being made and also on the time and equipment available. A good method of construction, resulting in a strong drawer which is neat in appearance, involves the use of lap, or rebate joints. This joint is used for both front corner joints, the back of the drawer being housed into the drawer sides. The plywood or hardboard base is grooved into the sides and front and is secured by screwing or nailing up into the drawer back from underneath. A development of this construction method will produce a drawer front which is wider than the drawer box itself. The advantage of this is that the space between the drawer and the cabinet side is hidden, giving a neater appearance to the unit. Also shown in the diagram is the use of the stopped housing to neaten the fitting of the back.

A much simpler drawer construction method consists of using butt joints at all four corners of the basic box, the base being fitted by nailing and glueing plywood or hardboard onto the underside of the box. To improve the appearance from the front a flush fitting or overlapping drawer front is fixed by screwing through the box front from the inside. At the other extreme is the traditional method of drawer construction which involves the cutting of dovetail joints. The joints at the front corners are lap dovetails, which do not show from the front, and the joints on the back corners are common or through dovetails. The base is usually grooved into the drawer sides and front and is secured by screwing up into the drawer back. It is common for the drawer front to be made of a thicker and better quality material than the drawer sides and back, and in some cases the sides may allow only a shallow groove to be cut. In such a situation, the support given by a shallow groove can be supplemented by glueing and pinning supporting strips of wood underneath the drawer bottom, or a separate grooved wooden strip can be fitted inside the drawer box. This latter method has the advantage of eliminating the need to groove the drawer sides and front.

The traditional method of drawer construction is best suited to a drawer made of solid timber, whereas the other methods lend themselves to the use of manufactured board materials. The sides and back of the drawers could be made of 12mm ($\frac{1}{2}$in) plywood and the front of veneered or melamine-faced chipboard. Again,

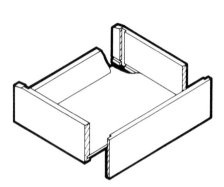

Drawer constructed with lap, or rebate joints and housing joints

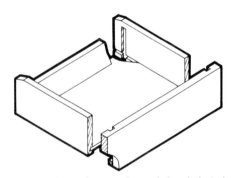

Separate drawer front may be attached to the basic drawer box

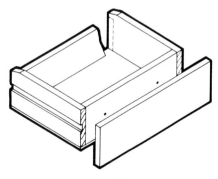

Simple butt jointed drawer box

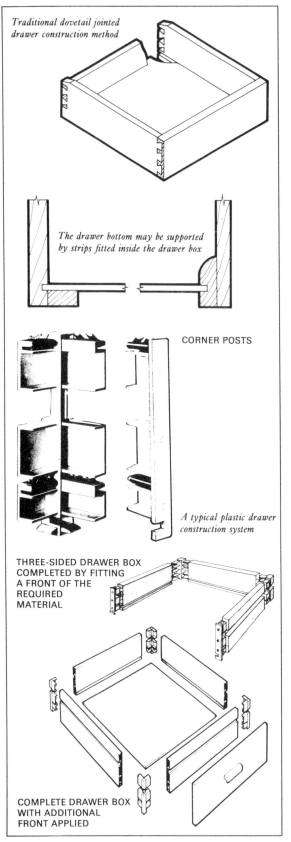

Traditional dovetail jointed drawer construction method

The drawer bottom may be supported by strips fitted inside the drawer box

CORNER POSTS

A typical plastic drawer construction system

THREE-SIDED DRAWER BOX
COMPLETED BY FITTING
A FRONT OF THE
REQUIRED
MATERIAL

COMPLETE DRAWER BOX
WITH ADDITIONAL
FRONT APPLIED

the choice will depend very much on the job in hand.

A fairly recent development has been the marketing of extruded plastic drawer-making systems which can make complete drawers, or can be used in conjunction with wooden fronts. No instructions can be given here as the systems all vary, but there is no doubt that they provide a quick and accurate method of drawer construction which might be particularly appropriate to the kitchen or bedroom.

There are further options when it comes to fitting the drawers into a cabinet, and consideration should be given to this when deciding on the drawer construction method itself. The simplest method of fitting is to provide an open-fronted space into which the drawer is a tight fit. This can be produced by fitting a complete shelf inside the cabinet or by fitting front and side rails which will support the drawer. If the drawer sides are thick enough to have a groove ploughed along them the drawer may be fitted by hanging it on runners. These runners are narrow strips of hardwood screwed into the cabinet sides and are planed to be slightly narrower than the width of the groove.

Provided that the necessary gap between the drawer and cabinet sides has been allowed for, the use of metal mechanical runners will ensure a smooth action and a considerable load carrying advantage. The runners have nylon wheels which provide smooth and silent operation and there is an in-built stop which prevents the drawer being opened too far. These runners are extremely easy to fit and the larger models allow loads up to 40kg to be pulled out completely clear of the cabinet. They are consequently very useful for applications such as the drawers of filing cabinets. When a drawer is being mounted under a table top, L-shaped runners can be made up of two strips of wood and screwed to the underside of the surface. Strips of wood of an appropriate size are screwed to the sides of the drawer to slide along the runners, and in this way the drawer may be suspended.

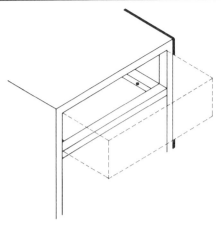

The drawer may be supported by a shelf or fitted frame

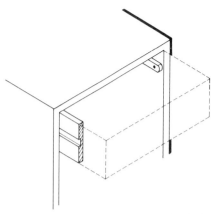

A drawer with grooves ploughed along the sides is fitted onto runners mounted inside the cabinet

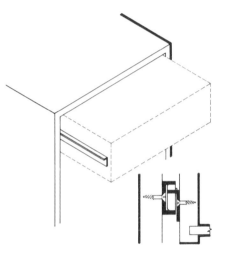

Mechanical runners ensure smooth action and have a considerable load carrying capacity

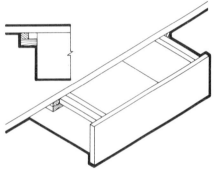

A drawer may be simply mounted under a work surface or table top

18 Hinges and hardware

There is available an almost bewildering variety of hinges and hardware items, and it can sometimes be difficult to know which type of hinge or fitting is best suited to a particular job. The items presented here can only be a selection and will hopefully cover the needs of most furniture-making undertakings.

The most common type of hinge is the butt hinge, which is available in brass or steel and in a wide range of sizes. This hinge is used for hinging jobs on all scales, from the fitting of a jewellery box lid to the hanging of a door. When buying the smaller sizes of brass hinge there is often a choice of a solid drawn or folded version. The solid drawn hinge, which is machined in solid brass, will be more expensive than the hinge made by folding sheet material, but it is a far superior hinge and is recommended for quality work.

FITTING A BUTT HINGE

The length of the hinge is carefully measured with a steel rule and marked out in the correct position with a knife and try square. The measurements for the width and depth of the hinge recesses are taken from the hinge itself with a marking gauge and the gauge is used to mark out these measurements on the wood between the lines which set out the hinge length. If the hinge is being fitted where appearance is not of paramount importance, a recess of uniform depth is easier to cut, but on a quality box or piece of furniture a tapered recess is preferred.

Angled sawcuts are made at both ends of the hinge recess with a tenon or dovetail saw, care being taken not to saw beyond the lines. Using a sharp chisel and striking it with a mallet, vertical cuts are made every few millimetres to segment the waste. In doing this it is best to work from the centre outwards with the grinding bevel of the chisel pointing towards the centre. Using scrapwood to support the material if necessary, the waste material is removed by careful horizontal paring until the recess has been completely opened out. The hinge is fitted into the recess and pilot holes made with a bradawl through the holes in the hinge, to prepare for the screws. It is normal practice to fit only the central screw and test that all is well before completing the fixing of the hinge. In this way adjustments can be made where necessary without having to fill unwanted screw holes.

If the hinge is to be fitted with brass screws it is recommended that slightly shorter steel screws be used first, to be withdrawn and replaced by the brass screws. The reason for this is that the slot in the head of a brass screw is easily damaged, especially when driving into hardwood, and the fitting of a steel screw first will cut a path through the wood for the brass screw to follow.

There are two common faults to avoid in the fitting of a hinge. Firstly, if the recesses are too shallow, or if the screw heads are too large, the door or lid will not be able to close fully. Secondly, if the recesses are too deep the closing of the door or lid will pull the screws and loosen them.

When hanging the doors of a cupboard or wardrobe it is important to use the correct number of hinges to give the required support. Obviously the size and weight of the door are important factors in deciding how many hinges should be used, but a general guide for doors up to 610mm (24in) wide would be two hinges on a door up to 1m ($39\frac{1}{4}$in) in height and one extra hinge for each additional 500mm ($19\frac{3}{4}$in) in height. It will be appreciated that it is better to err on the generous side when calculating the number of hinges required for a door.

There are two other hinges which are versions of the butt hinge and which are used in table construction, when fitting falling flaps. The back flap hinge is recessed into the underside of the table top and flap by a similar method to that just described for the butt hinge, and when fitted will allow the flap to fall into a vertical position or even to be folded through 180° to lie underneath the table top itself. The table leaf hinge is normally used in conjunction with a rule joint to make an extremely neat joint between the table top and flap, in both the opened out and folded positions. When compared with other hinges the table leaf hinge is countersunk on the opposite side, and when fitted the knuckle itself is recessed into the table top.

If a falling flap is to be fitted to a unit or wall to make a working surface in the kitchen or a writing surface in a bedroom there are a number of self-locking folding brackets which would be suitable. These brackets are available in white epoxy finish and are used in pairs to provide a firm working surface which can be folded down and out of the way when not required.

There are many versions of the concealed hinge that has become so popular with furniture manufacturers. The main advantages of this type of hinge are that it is

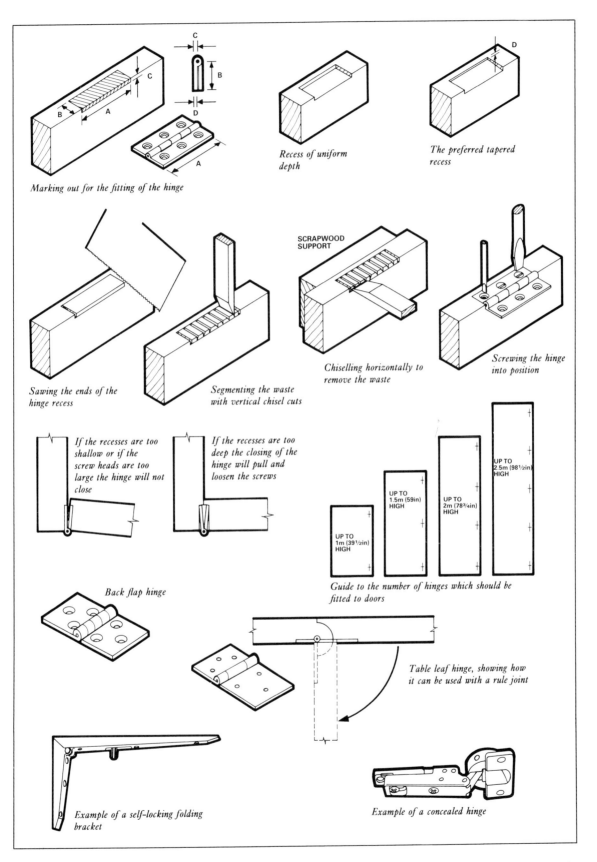

Marking out for the fitting of the hinge

Recess of uniform depth

The preferred tapered recess

Sawing the ends of the hinge recess

Segmenting the waste with vertical chisel cuts

SCRAPWOOD SUPPORT

Chiselling horizontally to remove the waste

Screwing the hinge into position

If the recesses are too shallow or if the screw heads are too large the hinge will not close

If the recesses are too deep the closing of the hinge will pull and loosen the screws

UP TO 1m (39½in) HIGH

UP TO 1.5m (59in) HIGH

UP TO 2m (78¾in) HIGH

UP TO 2.5m (98½in) HIGH

Guide to the number of hinges which should be fitted to doors

Back flap hinge

Table leaf hinge, showing how it can be used with a rule joint

Example of a self-locking folding bracket

Example of a concealed hinge

easy to fit and once in place is adjustable to allow the best possible fit to be achieved. The hinges are fitted into 35mm ($1\frac{3}{8}$in) diameter blind holes drilled near the edge of the door and onto mounting plates which are fitted inside the cabinet. There are three adjustments which can be made on some models by tightening or loosening screws on the mounting plates. Side adjustment is achieved with screw A, depth adjustment with screw B and height adjustment with screw C. The three main types of concealed hinge give different opening angles of 95°, 110° and 170° and these opening angles are clearly demonstrated in the adjustment illustrations. Concealed hinges are also available in sprung and locking versions as well as those with free movement.

A further type of hinge which is suitable for hanging cupboard or wardrobe doors and which is extremely easy to fit is the lay-on hinge. This hinge is available in sprung and unsprung versions and is simply screwed into place.

There are a number of hinges made of folded metal which do not require recesses and are fitted by screwing onto the surface of the cabinet and door. These hinges are particularly suitable for hanging the doors of kitchen base units and wall cabinets made of melamine-faced chipboard materials. The flush hinge and the single cranked hinge can be used on both inset and overlapping doors and permit 180° opening. The double cranked hinge allows 270° opening and is the strongest flush hinge. A further hinge in this category is the piano hinge, which is available in continuous lengths up to 1m 800mm (71in). The hinge, which is usually brass plated, is just cut to length and once screwed into place will allow 180° opening.

A hinge which may be used in similar circumstances as the piano hinge, when fitting flaps which must be open through 180°, is the radiused hinge. Its main advantage is that it is neat in appearance when the flap is folded, whereas the piano hinge is rather unattractive in this position.

A recent development has been the introduction of the cylinder hinge which is available in diameters of 10, 12, 14 and 16mm ($\frac{3}{8}$, $\frac{1}{2}$, $\frac{9}{16}$ and $\frac{5}{8}$in), to suit different thicknesses of material. The hinge is fitted into drilled holes and is extremely versatile as it can be used on inset or applied doors and falling flaps, and also on folding tops as it opens through a full 180°. This facility allows the construction of folding doors with these hinges which are completely invisible when in the closed position.

A hinge which may be more suitable for larger folding doors or screens is the brass Paravent screen hinge which permits 180° opening in both directions. The hinge is designed to be fitted to panels of 25mm (1in) in thickness and is screwed into place.

Another invisible hinge which is used to hang doors is the Soss hinge which is fully recessed into mortises, cut into the door and stile. It operates through a number of

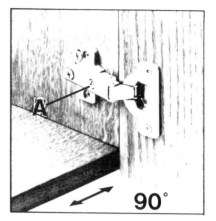

The adjustments which are possible with concealed hinges

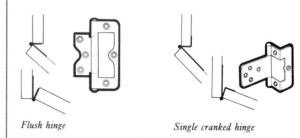

Flush hinge　　　　　　　　*Single cranked hinge*

Double cranked hinge

Radiused hinge

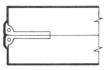

Cylinder hinges are available in a variety of diameters

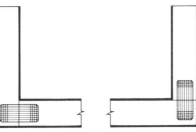

Sprung lay-on hinge. It is available in an unsprung version

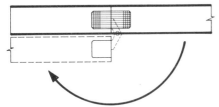

Cylinder hinges may be used on inset doors left or applied doors right and falling flaps

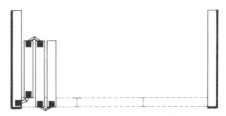

The hinge may also be used on folding tops

Folding doors can be constructed with cylinder hinges

Paravent screen hinge

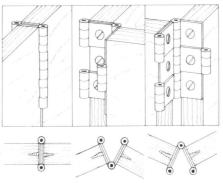

Paravent screen hinge

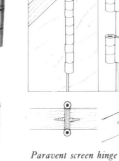

Soss hinge is fully recessed

Nylon peglock catch

Plastic roller catch

Example of a magnetic catch

Mini auto-latch

Magnetic touch latch

linked levers and is very strong and able to open through 180°

Hardware items that are concerned with the making of joints have already been dealt with in Ch. 12, and the items here are probably better described as cabinet fittings. A common requirement is the need to keep a door or flap securely closed and there are many catches available to fulfill this need. A strong locking action is provided by the peglock catch which is produced in white nylon and is particularly suitable for kitchen cupboard doors. The plastic roller catch has a smoother and quieter action but still provides a strong locking force and would perhaps be suitable for bedroom cupboard doors. The magnetic catch is now a common fitting and has the advantage of being easy to fit and fairly quiet in use, but it does not have the holding force of the mechanical catches previously described. There are two other catches which share the advantage of making handles unnecessary on doors. The mini auto-latch and the magnetic touch latch will both release the door when it is gently pushed in. The smoothness of this action and the fact that a striking plate is easily fitted to a glass door has made the magnetic touch latch a popular fitting on hi-fi towers with glass doors. The furniture bolt is a useful locking device in situations where double doors overlap one another down the centre, e.g. wardrobe doors. The bolt is used to secure the first door before the second door is closed against it.

Another common requirement is the need to control the movement of fall flaps and lift-up flaps. There are many stays on the market but two will answer most needs. The adjustable braking stay will control the movement of a fall flap and hold it firmly in a horizontal position. The braking action can be adjusted to suit the size and weight of flap and the stays would usually be fitted in pairs. The top box stay will control the movement of a lift-up flap and lock it in an open position. The lock is disengaged by raising the flap slightly before closing.

Mirror plates are a useful means of fixing frames to the wall. The plates are often brass-plated and are screwed to the back of the frame with two screws. This leaves one screw hole through which a wall fixing is made. There are two alternative designs of mirror plate; one with a hole for permanent wall fixing and the other with a keyhole slot so that the frame can be lifted from the wall.

When fixing a solid wood table top to an underframe a fitting is required which will allow for the movement of the timber. This movement will take place in response to changes in humidity and is across the grain. Shrinkage plates are fitted into recesses cut into the top rails and the two different plates must be positioned so that the slots lie across the grain. The top is fixed by screwing up through the plates with round head screws. An alternative design of shrinkage plate is screwed to the inside of the top rails and has slots cut in both directions,

the top being screwed on through the appropriate slot.

It is often desirable to make items of furniture more mobile by fitting glides or castors. Furniture glides are most suitable for cabinets which may have to be moved occasionally or easy chairs and settees, where they will allow the pieces to be moved quite easily but will not cause the chairs to move around as someone sits down or gets up. Ball, wheel or roller castors are useful for making trolleys and cabinets easily mobile and may be fitted with a peg and socket fixing or screwed in position through a plate fixing. (Normally peg and socket castors are fitted into end grain and plate castors fitted across the grain.) When choosing a castor it is important to ensure that the castor is able to support the weight of not only the piece of furniture but also the contents or load that it will contain or support.

Extruded sliding door channels provide a simple means of fitting glass, perspex or wooden doors up to 5mm ($\frac{3}{16}$in) thick. The channel is glued or screwed into place and the deeper channel must be fitted at the top to allow the doors to be pushed up and dropped down into the lower channel.

All sorts of handles for doors or drawers may be found in wood, plastic, metal and ceramic materials and most often these are fitted by screwing through from the inside of the door or drawer. Two other types of handle deserve a mention as they are fitted in a secure, but discreet way. Extruded plastic or aluminium handle strips are available in a variety of sections, some of which are suitable for fixing to the bottom of wall cabinet doors and others which are designed for the top of base unit doors. The handle strip is cut to length and the barbed spine should be a tight fit into a groove cut into the door edge. This groove should be stopped at both ends, which is quite possible with a slot cutter, and the handle spine must be trimmed accordingly. Wooden handles and mouldings which are fitted in the same way are also available. The second handle type is a shaped wooden block which is glued into a recess cut into the drawer or door. The handle may be chosen to match, or contrast, with the wood which has been used to make the item of furniture.

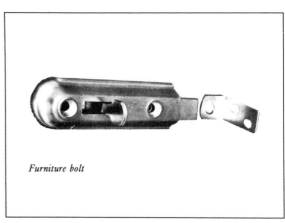

Furniture bolt

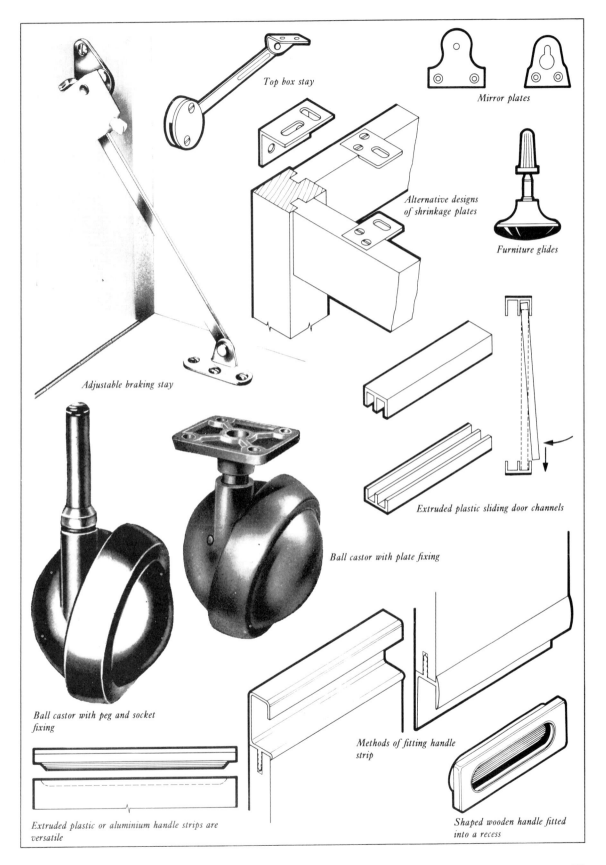

Top box stay

Mirror plates

Adjustable braking stay

Alternative designs
of shrinkage plates

Furniture glides

Extruded plastic sliding door channels

Ball castor with plate fixing

Ball castor with peg and socket
fixing

Methods of fitting handle
strip

Extruded plastic or aluminium handle strips are
versatile

Shaped wooden handle fitted
into a recess

19 Upholstery techniques

Polyether foam is the material which is best used for making comfortable cushions or shaped surfaces, for sitting or lying on, and it is available in a number of grades and thicknesses. The grades of foam have different densities and the success of using the material depends on choosing the correct grade and thickness. The grades of polyether foam made by Dunlop are Dunlopreme D1 to D17 and a general guide to their use is given. Within the basic categories of usage the higher the grade of foam that is used the better.

D1–D8: Can be used for back cushions, headrests and arms.

D10–D17: Can be used for seating cushions.

The thickness of foam required for a particular job will depend on the base or platform material against which the foam will operate. On a rigid baseboard a foam cushion should be of a firm grade and at least 90mm ($3\frac{1}{2}$in) thick. If a softer grade is to be substituted a thickness of at least 120mm ($4\frac{3}{4}$in) is necessary. When elastic webbing or rubber platforms are the means of support, the firmer grades can be reduced to 70–80mm ($2\frac{3}{4}$–$3\frac{1}{4}$in), and the softer grades to 100mm (4in), but this will not give comfort if the cushion rests on a rail or solid frame support. If there is no way of avoiding such contact the rail or frame member should be padded.

If the thicknesses stated are considered to be too bulky for a particular piece of furniture, the overall thickness can be reduced by laminating different grades of foam together, e.g. a 120mm ($4\frac{3}{4}$in) cushion of a softer grade may be reduced to 100mm (4in) in thickness by laminating 70mm ($2\frac{3}{4}$in) of the softer grade with 30mm ($1\frac{1}{4}$in) of a firmer grade. This combination of foam types can often result in a more satisfactory seating cushion, as precisely the correct amount of surface comfort can be combined with sufficient in-depth support. Laminations can also help to achieve a wide variety of seating shapes and this is dealt with in some detail later in the section.

When cutting the foam it is important to achieve accuracy and clean surfaces. Any fine-toothed saw will cut the material successfully, ideally a bandsaw with an appropriate blade. In the absence of such a machine an electric carving knife will make an excellent cut in the material with little effort, but equally a hacksaw blade or bread knife can be used. The use of templates is recommended when cutting shapes like circles, especially if the same shape is to be repeated a number of times. The templates are easily prepared from card or hardboard and should be wired together on both sides of the foam. Foam should always be cut slightly oversize so that when it is covered with fabric it is held under slight compression. A slab of foam the size of a mattress should be cut 20mm ($\frac{3}{4}$in) oversize in length and 15mm ($\frac{5}{8}$in) in width. Seating cushions will need an extra 5mm ($\frac{3}{16}$in) or so in length and width and an extra 10% should be allowed for in thickness.

Sometimes a seating requirement can be satisfied by a flat slab of foam, but usually some form of shaping is desirable. There are a number of ways of achieving seating shapes and a good adhesive is essential to all of them, to join the foam to a base or to itself. The contact adhesive Thixofix, made by Dunlop, is strongly recommended as it makes extremely good bonds and, being thixotropic, is economical in use. To curve the edge of a cushion the edge of the foam is chamfered by cutting against straight edges. The chamfered edge is then glued down to the base and in this way a smooth curve is formed. If a round edge is required on a loose cushion a shallow V channel should be cut into the edge of the foam. This channel is then glued and closed to form the rounded edge. To make a domed cushion shape two layers of foam which are each half of the cushion thickness are glued together with a third piece of foam sandwiched between them. The foam in the middle needs to be about 30mm ($1\frac{1}{4}$in) thick and 90mm ($3\frac{1}{2}$in) smaller all around than the outer pieces. This principle can be used to great effect for the construction of back and headrest panels. In doing this type of work a series of experiments would be carried out to decide the lamination required.

With seating cushions there is often a lack of support on the front edge and an extra thickness of foam is really required to give adequate leg support. This can be achieved by adding a strip of firm foam to the cushion and covering it with a thin and soft wrap or, alternatively, a foam strip can be put under the main seat cushion at the front. Arm shapes are also produced by laminating different grades and thicknesses of foam, firmer blocks of foam usually being wrapped with thinner and softer foam. The important factor here is that the arm rest should be able to resist elbow pressure without bottoming, i.e. without the base being felt through the support. If the backs of chairs are to be buttoned a 30mm ($1\frac{1}{4}$in) layer of soft foam should be

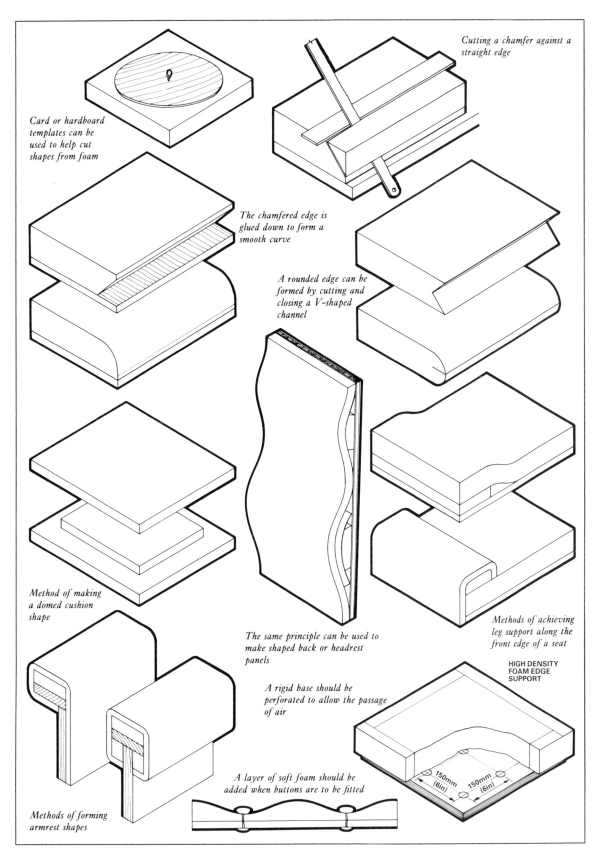

Card or hardboard templates can be used to help cut shapes from foam

Cutting a chamfer against a straight edge

The chamfered edge is glued down to form a smooth curve

A rounded edge can be formed by cutting and closing a V-shaped channel

Method of making a domed cushion shape

The same principle can be used to make shaped back or headrest panels

Methods of achieving leg support along the front edge of a seat

A rigid base should be perforated to allow the passage of air

HIGH DENSITY FOAM EDGE SUPPORT

Methods of forming armrest shapes

A layer of soft foam should be added when buttons are to be fitted

150mm (6in)   150mm (6in)

75

added to the basic foam slab required, but for a buttoned headboard or bedhead a 40mm (1½in) layer of soft foam stuck to the backing board is sufficient.

When the foam is to be fixed to a rigid base, provision must be made for the passage of air that is necessary for the foam to compress and re-inflate. The base should be drilled with 20mm (¾in) holes at 150mm (6in) centres to allow for this and it is particularly important to do this if the foam is to be upholstered with a material which does not breathe e.g. P.V.C. Also shown in the diagram is a method of providing firm edge support to a seating cushion by glueing strips of a high density foam around the edge.

Pirelli resilient webbing is a popular method of providing a comfortable seat platform. The webbing strands should run from front to back and the gaps left between strands should be no more than the width of the strands themselves. The webbing is produced in a range of widths and to different specifications but the figures given relate to the most common 51mm (2in) wide standard webbing. The figure for the seat span should be taken to be the distance between the fixing grooves, staples or tacks.

seat span	strand length
457mm (18in)	432mm (17in)
483mm (19in)	457mm (18in)
508mm (20in)	483mm (19in)
533mm (21in)	508mm (20in)
559mm (22in)	521mm (20½in)
584mm (23in)	546mm (21½in)
610mm (24in)	571mm (22½in)

These figures for the strand length would give a medium seating hardness. For a softer seating requirement add 13mm (½in) and for a harder seat subtract 13mm (½in) from the strand length

The neatest and most secure method of fitting the webbing strands uses the steel clips which are supplied. These clips are simply closed onto the ends of the strands and fitted into a 4mm (5/32in) wide 15mm (5/8in) deep groove cut into the frame at an angle of 75° to the horizontal. The webbing can, however, be tacked or stapled onto the rails, provided that great care is taken not to allow a tear to develop in the webbing as a result of inserting the staples too hard or driving a tack in at an angle. The end of the webbing can be hidden by fixing it into a shallow rebate, but most often the webbing is fitted into grooved pieces of wood which are screwed into the backs of the front and back rails. This not only hides the webbing but also provides a lip to contain the foam cushion which would be used for the seat. It should be noted that the inside edge of the wood onto which the webbing is fixed must be rounded so that the webbing does not come into contact with a sharp edge when under load.

The Pirelli four-point platform provides a good seating platform and is extremely easy to fit. It is important that the platform operates under the correct tension, and consequently it is necessary to design the dimensions of a piece of furniture around the figures in the table opposite. The stretched and unstretched measurements are taken from inside the triangular corner loops.

There are alternative methods for fixing the platform to a chair frame and two methods are described here. The barbed hook fits into a 13mm (½in) hole drilled to a depth of 18mm (¾in) in the side of the leg or side rail, and is held at the correct angle by a plastic plug which is pushed over the hook. Another method involves the use of the mushroom-headed rivets which are available for top fixing. These rivets are driven into 6.3mm (¼in) holes drilled to a depth of 51mm (2in) into the top of a leg, corner block or rail. The surface which takes the rivet must be chamfered to between 15° and 20° to permit the movement of the corner loop.

The fabric or material that is chosen to upholster a particular piece of furniture depends on the appearance and wearing characteristics required. There is a wide range of upholstery materials which includes linen, heavy woollen and synthetic mixtures, stretch nylon, P.V.C. coated knitted fabric, leather and velours, in particular Dralon.

If a cushion cover is to be removed regularly or if an open weave material is being used for the covering an undercover of calico should be made and fitted. For a fixed cushion the calico may be glued or taped to the frame itself, but on a loose cushion it should be a complete envelope. It is also recommended that a layer of Dacron be used on top of the foam to give a soft and rounded look to the cushion. It is obviously advisable to fit a zip into covers which are to be removed for cleaning, or else Velcro touch-and-close fastener may be used. Velcro can also be used to hold loose cushions in place by fixing one tape to the cusion and the second to the frame.

A common upholstering situation is the covering of a flat slab of foam on a rigid base. The size of the material is calculated and marked out by adding the widths required for the thickness of the foam, the thickness of the base and the amount for turning under, onto the size of the base. (The width allowed for the thickness of the foam will be the actual thickness minus 10%.) The four corners of the material are sewn with the material turned inside out and the bulk of the waste cut off. The box which results is then turned right side out and fitted over the foam and base. The cover is then turned under the base and stapled or tacked on, working from the centres of the sides towards the corners. The corners themselves should be carefully folded to avoid an unsightly bulk before being stapled or tacked.

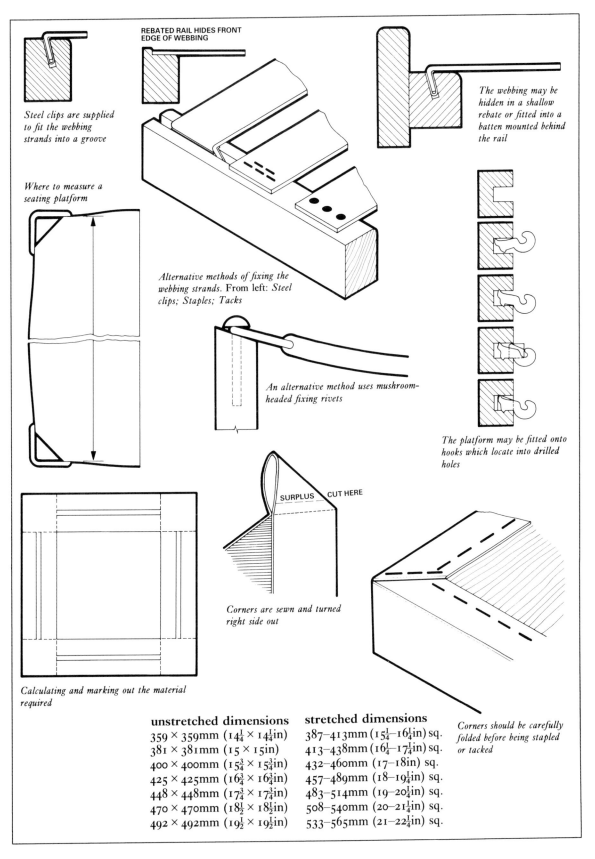

REBATED RAIL HIDES FRONT
EDGE OF WEBBING

Steel clips are supplied
to fit the webbing
strands into a groove

The webbing may be
hidden in a shallow
rebate or fitted into a
batten mounted behind
the rail

Where to measure a
seating platform

Alternative methods of fixing the
webbing strands. From left: Steel
clips; Staples; Tacks

An alternative method uses mushroom-
headed fixing rivets

The platform may be fitted onto
hooks which locate into drilled
holes

SURPLUS   CUT HERE

Corners are sewn and turned
right side out

Calculating and marking out the material
required

unstretched dimensions
359×359mm ($14\frac{1}{4} \times 14\frac{1}{4}$in)
381×381mm (15×15in)
400×400mm ($15\frac{3}{4} \times 15\frac{3}{4}$in)
425×425mm ($16\frac{3}{4} \times 16\frac{3}{4}$in)
448×448mm ($17\frac{3}{4} \times 17\frac{3}{4}$in)
470×470mm ($18\frac{1}{2} \times 18\frac{1}{2}$in)
492×492mm ($19\frac{1}{2} \times 19\frac{1}{2}$in)

stretched dimensions
$387-413$mm ($15\frac{1}{4}-16\frac{1}{4}$in) sq.
$413-438$mm ($16\frac{1}{4}-17\frac{1}{4}$in) sq.
$432-460$mm ($17-18$in) sq.
$457-489$mm ($18-19\frac{1}{4}$in) sq.
$483-514$mm ($19-20\frac{1}{4}$in) sq.
$508-540$mm ($20-21\frac{1}{4}$in) sq.
$533-565$mm ($21-22\frac{1}{4}$in) sq.

Corners should be carefully
folded before being stapled
or tacked

77

20 Working acrylic sheet

Acrylic sheet is a common manufacturing material but its potential for making items for the home is perhaps not fully appreciated. The material is most useful in sheet form and it is produced in a range of opaque and translucent colours, as well as clear. The sheet thicknesses which are most useful for home use are 3mm and 5mm ($\frac{1}{8}$in and $\frac{3}{16}$in). Using the correct Tensol cements, e.g. I.C.I Tensol cement No.12, fabrications can be made up with flat acrylic sheet, but more useful shapes can be achieved through a variety of relatively simple forming techniques. All of these techniques require the sheet material to be heated to 150°–170°C (302°–338°F) and this can easily be done in a domestic oven, provided that the setting required to give this temperature is established. Once the acrylic has been moulded to shape it may prove rather difficult to work on, and there is the danger of cracking the moulding. For this reason all drilling, shaping and edge trimming should be carried out before moulding, as far as is possible. The acrylic sheet is put in the oven towards the top on a baking tray or wire mesh for support. The oven should be preheated to the required temperature. Gloves will be needed to remove the heated sheet from the oven and to place it onto the moulding apparatus. Pressure should be kept on the acrylic until it has cooled sufficiently to retain the shape to which it has been formed, and the temptation to speed up this cooling by using water should be avoided, as this can set up stresses in the material and make it brittle.

To cut acrylic sheet to size any fine-toothed saw can be used. For straight cuts on large sheets a tenon saw or dovetail saw will make a perfectly good cut, but it is important to ensure that the sheet is well supported. An electric jig saw or bandsaw fitted with a fine-toothed blade can be used on the material and would be particularly useful for the cutting of curves. If only hand tools are available curves are cut with a pad saw or coping saw. The material can be drilled with normal twist drills, but when using larger sizes of drill a slow speed should be selected to minimise the amount of heat generated. The acrylic should be cramped down onto a piece of scrapwood for drilling and particular care should be taken as the drill breaks through the far side, as it is at this point that grabbing and breakage is most likely to occur. The edges of acrylic material can be planed smooth with a sharp and finely-set woodworking plane and this will be found to be a quicker method of removing waste material than by filing. Intricate shapes, however, will have to be filed with the appropriate file, the tool being moved along the edge as it is pushed forward on the cutting stroke. Wet or dry abrasive papers are the best materials for rubbing down the surfaces of acrylic before polishing, and by carefully working through the grades the work required in the polishing stage can be greatly reduced. Conventional polishing compounds, e.g. liquid metal polishes, can be used to bring the worked surface to a high gloss by hand polishing with a cloth.

There are a number of techniques which can be used to produce single curvature bends in acrylic sheet. A right-angled bend with a radiused corner can be made over a former which consists of two pieces of board with a supporting corner block. The pressure needed to hold the heated sheet in position is applied through two further pieces of board which are hinged with a strip of canvas, tacked into place. If a sharper bend is required a different method can be employed whereby pairs of battens are fitted to the acrylic sheet either side of the bending line, before the sheet is heated. The top battens are planed to an angle which is half of the angle of the final bend, e.g. 45° for a right-angled bend, and the battens on the underside are positioned so that a gap is left to allow the acrylic to be thoroughly heated through. Once the moulding temperature has been reached, the bend is made and the internal battens will act as a stop when the correct angle is reached. When the acrylic has cooled the battens are removed and perhaps repositioned for a second bend. If this is the case some means will need to be devised to hold the first bend as acrylic sheet has a memory and will return to its original flat state unless it is held in position. When larger sheets are being formed by this method the battens on the underside should be replaced by boards to support the material under heat.

Bends which involve a large radius are best formed with matching formers, between which the heated acrylic is sandwiched. These formers can be made quite easily by cutting chipboard or blockboard pieces to shape and then lining the edges with cardboard or very thin plywood. Curved and almost circular forms can be pulled around a solid or box former with a length of cloth. If the ends of the cloth are wrapped around and tacked to dowel rods a more even pressure will be possible. If there is a danger of the texture of the cloth

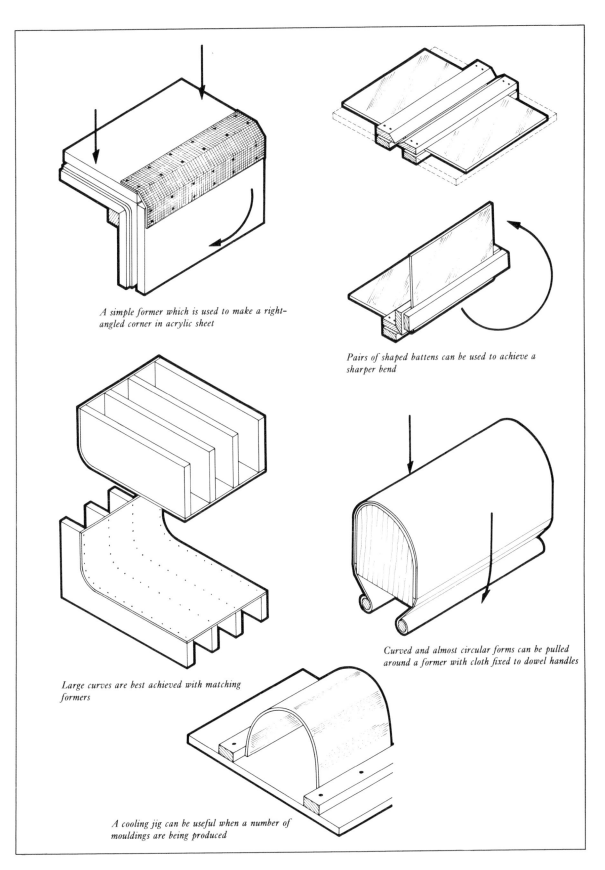

A simple former which is used to make a right-angled corner in acrylic sheet

Pairs of shaped battens can be used to achieve a sharper bend

Large curves are best achieved with matching formers

Curved and almost circular forms can be pulled around a former with cloth fixed to dowel handles

A cooling jig can be useful when a number of mouldings are being produced

being embossed into the hot acrylic a sheet of paper can be placed on the acrylic before the cloth is pulled over. For some shapes a cooling jig can be useful to save having to stand and hold the acrylic under pressure until it has totally cooled. A flat board with strips of wood nailed into position is all that is needed for this, and indeed such a jig could be used as a former for simple semi–circular shapes.

Shapes with a double curvature can also be formed but the formers will probably require more preparation. The acrylic, once heated, needs to be pressed and stretched into shape and the formers must therefore incorporate a clamping device to hold the edges of the material. The forming box illustrated was developed to produce acrylic light covers and the basic design would be suitable for a wide range of small mouldings. The heated acrylic is placed onto the lower half of the box and pressed over the nail points and then the top half of the former is lowered down. This action causes the shaped plug to push the sheet through the shaped aperture in the lower box half, making the moulding. The pressure necessary for this can be supplied simply by standing on the moulding box. The holes drilled through the sides of the top half of the former were found to be necessary as, on cooling, the acrylic shrinks onto the plug and is hard to remove. The holes allow a screwdriver to be used to lever the moulding from the former.

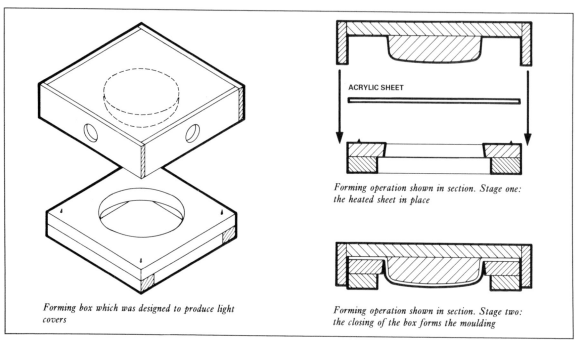

Forming box which was designed to produce light covers

ACRYLIC SHEET

Forming operation shown in section. Stage one: the heated sheet in place

Forming operation shown in section. Stage two: the closing of the box forms the moulding

21 Plans and preparation

When a piece of furniture is to be designed, the design solution will respond to a number of factors which arise out of the particular situation for which the design is being prepared. A list of these factors will commonly include entries such as suitability of materials, cost, method of construction, finish, etc., but an individual list of relevant factors will come out from each design project. In preparing a design it is obviously important to give consideration to these factors, and a successful design can perhaps be defined as the one which satisfies these requirements to the fullest extent. It will be appreciated that compromises often have to be made, and during the process of design the factors will attract a weighting which will have an effect on certain decisions that are made in arriving at a final design solution.

A major part of the preparation work is the task of putting dimensions to a design idea or concept and deciding on the section of material which will provide the necessary strength. It is hoped that help with the latter point can be obtained by looking through the design suggestions which follow, and guidance found by comparing the scale of work being undertaken with the examples given. The dimensioning of a piece of work will often involve consideration of the size and shape of the human body (anthropometrics) and also consideration of the relationship between the human body and its environment, e.g. comfortable seating positions, working areas and cupboard heights (ergonomics). There are no set formulae or fixed dimensions which must be adhered to but there are established guidelines which are the result of extensive research, and these provide a useful starting point. Three diagrams are provided which give a guide to the dimensions which may be required. The first deals with table height and seating height for a working desk, dining or kitchen table. The second also deals with table and seating height, but this time the furniture involved is lounge furniture, e.g. easy chairs and coffee or occasional tables. The third diagram gives a guide to the height of worktops and cupboards in a kitchen.

A design is usually arrived at through a series of sketches in which ideas are tested out against information that has been gathered through research and also against the functional and visual requirements. It is

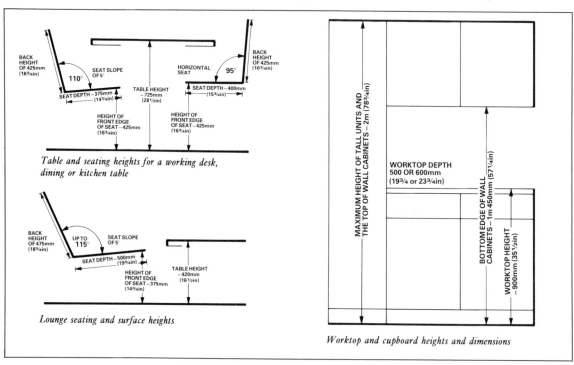

Table and seating heights for a working desk, dining or kitchen table

Lounge seating and surface heights

Worktop and cupboard heights and dimensions

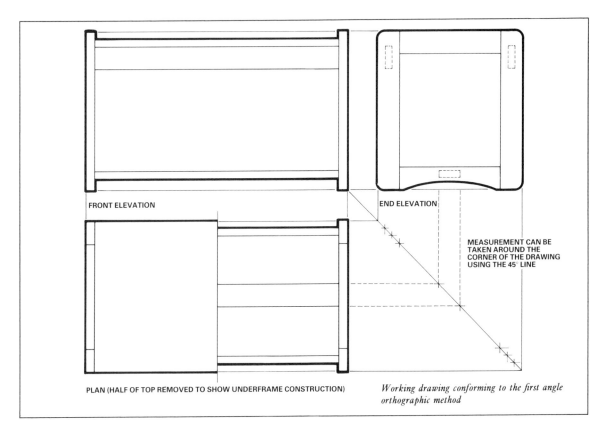

FRONT ELEVATION

END ELEVATION

MEASUREMENT CAN BE
TAKEN AROUND THE
CORNER OF THE DRAWING
USING THE 45° LINE

PLAN (HALF OF TOP REMOVED TO SHOW UNDERFRAME CONSTRUCTION)

Working drawing conforming to the first angle orthographic method

CUTTING LIST

description	material	length	width	thickness	no. off	comments
Vertical end frame members	Mahogany	420mm (16½in)	60mm (2¼in)	20mm (¾in)	4	End frames are dowel jointed
Horizontal end frame members	Mahogany	280mm (11in)	60mm (2¼in)	20mm (¾in)	4	Bottom members have curved underside
Rails	Mahogany	680mm (26¾in)	60mm (2¼in)	20mm (¾in)	3	Rails are dowel jointed to end frames
Top	Mahogany-faced chipboard	670mm (26½in)	390mm (15¼in)	16mm (⅝in)	1	Edged with solid mahogany lipping
Lipping	Mahogany	2m 200mm (86¾in)	20mm (¾in)	5mm (¼in)	1	Glued around top and planed flush

normal practice to make a measured working drawing of the design from which measurements can be taken, and the first angle orthographic method of drawing is the one most commonly used. By this drawing method three views of the piece of furniture are set out on paper, these being the front elevation, end elevation and plan view. If drawing equipment is available (drawing board, T square and set square) these views can be set out formally with the plan directly under the front elevation, and the end elevation adjacent to the front elevation. The oblique line which runs at 45° from the bottom right-hand corner of the front elevation allows measurements to be taken around the corner from the end elevation to the plan, or vice versa, and because the drawings are all in line with one another the measurements that have to be made to create the drawing are kept to a minimum, information being passed from one view to another with the T square and set square. If equipment is not available the views can be drawn individually and nothing will be lost. Ideally the working drawing would be full size, measurements could be taken directly from it during the making of the piece and completed items could be tested by laying them onto the drawing, but it is normally the case that a scale drawing has to be made. The scale which is to be used will obviously depend on the size of the design and the facilities at hand, but 1:2, 1:5 and 1:10 are accepted drawing scales.

It is from the working drawing that a cutting list can be prepared and a typical layout for such a list is illustrated for the occasional table shown in the working drawing. The sizes entered into the cutting list are finished sizes and when the timber is ordered and the pieces are roughly cut out allowances have to be made. When planing to width 4–5mm (about $\frac{1}{4}$in) extra material should be allowed for, 3mm ($\frac{1}{8}$in) or so should be allowed for when planing to thickness and up to 10mm ($\frac{3}{8}$in) when cutting to length. (If a horn is to be left above a joint this must be allowed for when ordering and subsequently cutting the timber.) The total lengths and areas of material are easily calculated from a cutting list and it is a useful sheet to work from in the initial stages of making an item.

Before committing time and money to buying materials and starting to make a piece of furniture it is advisable to test and evaluate the appearance and performance of the design as far as is possible. The isometric drawing method is a quick way of producing a three-dimensional view of an item. The method does not allow for any perspective and consequently there is a visual distortion within the drawing, but when drawing smaller items this is relatively unimportant. The drawing method is based on angles of 120° and the object is drawn with one vertical corner foremost in the drawing. Horizontal edges and surfaces on the actual item of furniture are drawn at 30° to the horizontal on the paper using a set square and the dimensions, or scaled measurements, are measured off along the lines.

Modelling in card or balsa wood is a further method of trying out an idea, and obviously any shortfalls discovered then can be remedied in the design. For some items of furniture it will be very important to test the design at full size in some way to check a seating position or a reaching height. Full size drawings or marks measured onto the wall can sometimes satisfy an enquiry, but the use of scrap materials to make mock-ups is highly recommended. The time spent in this activity should be regarded as an investment in terms of ensuring as far as is possible that the final product is successful.

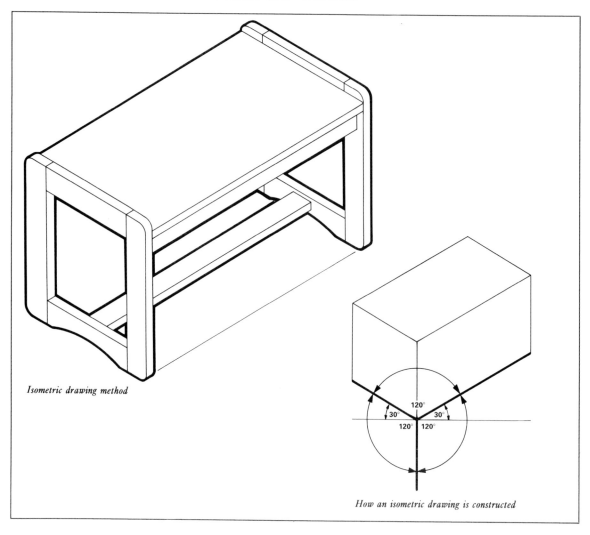

Isometric drawing method

How an isometric drawing is constructed

22 Shelving

The making and fitting of shelves is an activity which is relevant to most areas within the house and consequently deserving of a section of its own. The choice of which method to adopt for a particular situation will depend very much on the load-bearing capacity required and the importance of the visual appearance of the shelving in a specific location.

The shelf surfaces themselves can be of solid wood or manufactured board. If the shelf is to be narrow a single board can be used and this might be of softwood or hardwood. A suitable alternative to solid wood would be a veneered or melamine-faced chipboard panel of one of the narrower widths. A wider shelf requirement may make it necessary to edge-joint solid wood boards together and reinforce them by adding a deep edging piece on the front. A wider chipboard panel will probably require reinforcement in the form of supporting solid wood strips attached underneath the shelf, at the front and the back. The appearance of the shelf can be improved by the addition of an edging strip on the front. With very deep shelving there is the possibility of making a material economy in solid wood by using a series of thick, but narrow, lengths of wood, spaced apart at regular intervals. This will also eliminate the

warping problems that are associated with the making up of a large area of solid wood. Chipboard will not be suitable for the sort of loading that a deep shelf may have to take, blockboard being preferable. The board should be cut so that the core strips run along the length of the shelf and the front edge can be lipped with a strip of solid timber.

If a shelf is being fitted into an alcove it can be fixed down onto battens which have been plugged and screwed onto the wall. Care must be taken to position the battens level and it is normal practice to slant the ends of the side battens to make them less obtrusive. In situations where the battens are clearly visible their appearance can be improved by planing a low-angled chamfer along the bottom edge. A recent development has been the marketing of plastic alcove shelf supports, available in white or brown. The plastic support strips are secured to the underside of the shelf with four screws, at both ends. A jacking strip which has a moulded gripping surface locates into each support strip and jacking screws are screwed loosely into place. With the shelf held in the correct fitting position the jacking screws are turned and the jacking strips are forced outwards against the alcove sides. In this way the shelf is

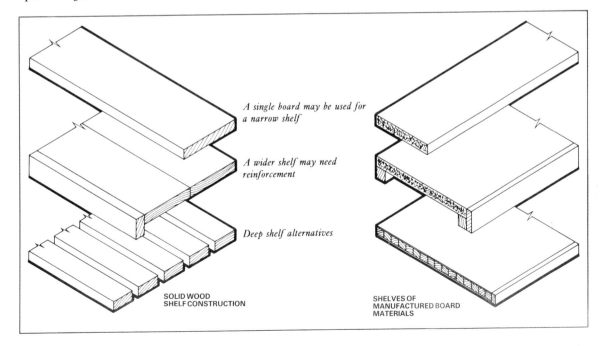

A single board may be used for a narrow shelf

A wider shelf may need reinforcement

Deep shelf alternatives

SOLID WOOD
SHELF CONSTRUCTION

SHELVES OF
MANUFACTURED BOARD
MATERIALS

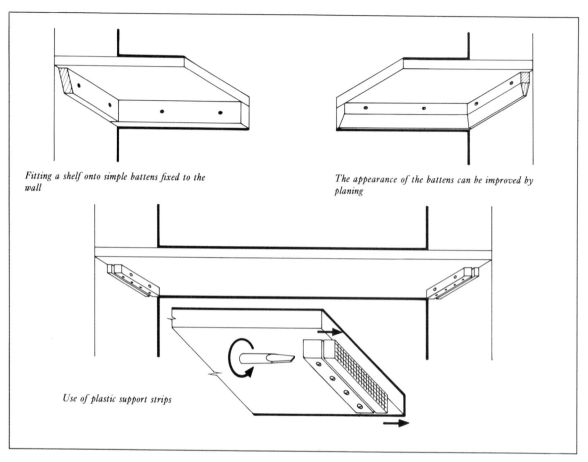

Fitting a shelf onto simple battens fixed to the wall

The appearance of the battens can be improved by planing

Use of plastic support strips

wedged firmly in position and is able to take a load of approximately 20kg (44lb).

The method of fitting shelving with battens can also be used to take shelves around corners and both internal and external corners can be accommodated, provided that the shelf is narrow.

When shelves are to be fitted to a flat wall a more elaborate construction is required. If a number of shelves is planned it is recommended that vertical battens are fixed to the wall, with the shelves fitted to the battens. A major advantage of this method is that the shelves will be distanced from the wall by the thickness of the battens, making it unnecessary to trim the back edges of the shelves to match the irregularities of the wall surface. If wood is to be used for the brackets which support the shelf, the same material as the wall battens can be used. The joints best suited to this bracket construction are notch joints, which are simple to cut but will give great strength to the frame. A simpler, but less attractive, solution has the horizontal support notched into the wall batten, but to hold the right angle a triangular piece of plywood is screwed, or glued and nailed, to the outer or inner edges of the timber. The appearance of the bracket could perhaps be improved by shaping the edge of the plywood and by cutting a hole through it to lessen its visual weight. Metal shelf

support brackets are available in a number of forms but often their appearance means they can only be used with shelving in the garage or workshop. There are some designs of bracket which are more attractive and come in a range of coloured finishes, although these are considerably more expensive.

When shelves are to be fitted inside bookcases or cupboards a decision has to be made whether the shelf needs to provide support to the cupboard construction or whether it is to be separate. If the shelf is to provide support to the construction by holding the cupboard sides together, the use of a housing joint should be considered if the construction material is solid wood; in the case of manufactured board, one of the K.D. fittings would be suitable. When shelves are to be fitted in the one position but will not be part of the actual constructional strength of the piece there are alternative methods of fixing, and appearance will be a major factor in deciding the method to be used. Plastic nail-in supports are perhaps the simplest way of holding a shelf and they can be used to support a shelf along its length, by positioning along the back edge, as well as at the ends. Wooden battens screwed to the cabinet sides will provide a strong shelf support, but their appearance may limit the usefulness of this method. An advantage, however, is that the shelf can be nailed or screwed down

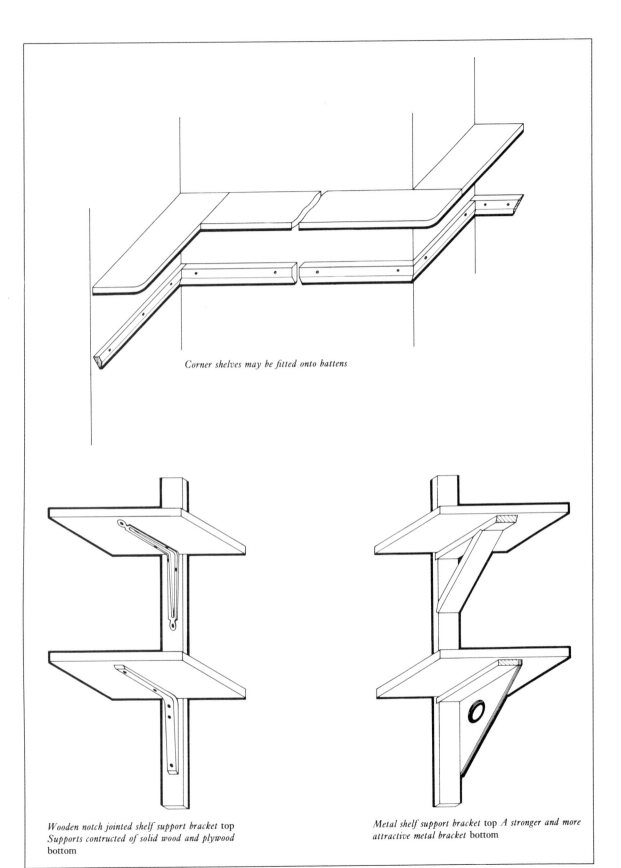

Corner shelves may be fitted onto battens

Wooden notch jointed shelf support bracket top
Supports contructed of solid wood and plywood
bottom

Metal shelf support bracket top *A stronger and more
attractive metal bracket* bottom

onto the batten to secure it. The plastic shelf bearer is a moulding which should be cut in half for narrow shelves or perhaps used in pairs for wider shelves. The bearers are simply screwed into place and the shelf must be cut 10mm ($\frac{3}{8}$in) shorter in length to take account of the thickness of the bearers.

Adjustable fittings for shelving obviously allow changes in shelf spacing to be made and again there are a number of available systems. The bookcase strip is usually available in 914mm (36in) lengths, with a plated zinc or bronze finish, and is surface-fitted with screws. The shelf support clips which are bought to match the strip are simply clipped into the horizontal slots to give the required shelf spacing and are very strong. A more discreet support system is provided by the nickel-plated flush fitting shelf support bracket and socket. The sockets are fitted into 7mm ($\frac{3}{8}$in) holes drilled at regular intervals inside the cabinet and the support brackets are fitted into the sockets at the desired heights. As the brackets are thin the shelf length only needs to be a little shorter than the internal width of the cabinet. There are a variety of plastic shelf supporting studs and fittings and two adjustable systems are illustrated. The upper diagram shows a shelf support which simply fits into 5mm ($\frac{3}{16}$in) holes drilled into the cabinet sides at regular intervals. The fitting has the advantage of gripping the shelf and holding it in position, which can be useful in kitchen and bedroom cupboard construction. The stud and bush shelf support is a simple but effective method of holding shelves. The bushes are normally fitted into regularly spaced holes and the studs inserted at the required heights.

The magic wire shelf fitting is a particularly neat and strong shelf fitting which can be used as a one-position fixing or as an adjustable system. The wires are available in a range of lengths to suit different shelf depths and are simply fitted into 3mm ($\frac{1}{8}$in) holes drilled into the cabinet sides. The shelf has to have a 9mm ($\frac{3}{8}$in) deep and 3mm ($\frac{1}{8}$in) wide groove cut along its ends to be able to slide over the wires and this groove should not come through to the front edge, but be stopped short so that it does not show. The groove is easily cut with a slot cutter which operates in a portable power drill fitted to a stand.

In addition to the methods previously described some further suggestions for solving shelving problems around the house are given here. Although the basic construction method is outlined the dimensions and materials which are chosen will depend on the situation. A shelf of solid wood or manufactured board may be hung from the wall by fitting end pieces and a horizontal rail, through which the wall fixing is made. The joint between the end piece and the shelf should be a housing and the technique of disguising a through housing by fitting a wider shelf is shown. The joints between the rail and the end pieces need to be strong, as it is these joints which hold the weight of the shelf plus its load. In solid wood these joints could be lap dovetails, but equally

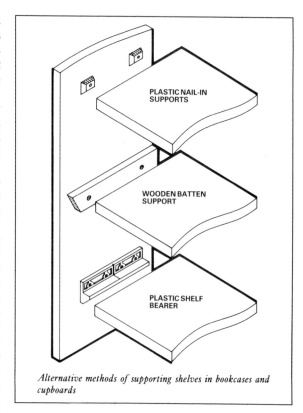

Alternative methods of supporting shelves in bookcases and cupboards

dowel joints would be suitable for all materials. An alternative end treatment is to bring the shelf beyond the end piece to make a separate surface for ornaments. In this case the joint between the end piece and the shelf should be a cross-halving (only half of the width of the end piece is taken from each piece), and in thick solid timber a greater strength and a neater appearance can be achieved by using the elaborated version of the cross-halving shown in Ch. 4.

The semi-circular shelf design is particularly suited to veneered or melamine-faced chipboard and would be well positioned by the bed. Dowel joints would be used for the construction of the shelf and if the curves are smooth and the edges kept square there will be no problem in covering the edges with iron-on strip to match the board material. Two screws are sufficient to fix the shelf to the wall.

Using the batten fixing method, attractively shaped corner shelves of a surprisingly large area can be securely mounted on the wall.

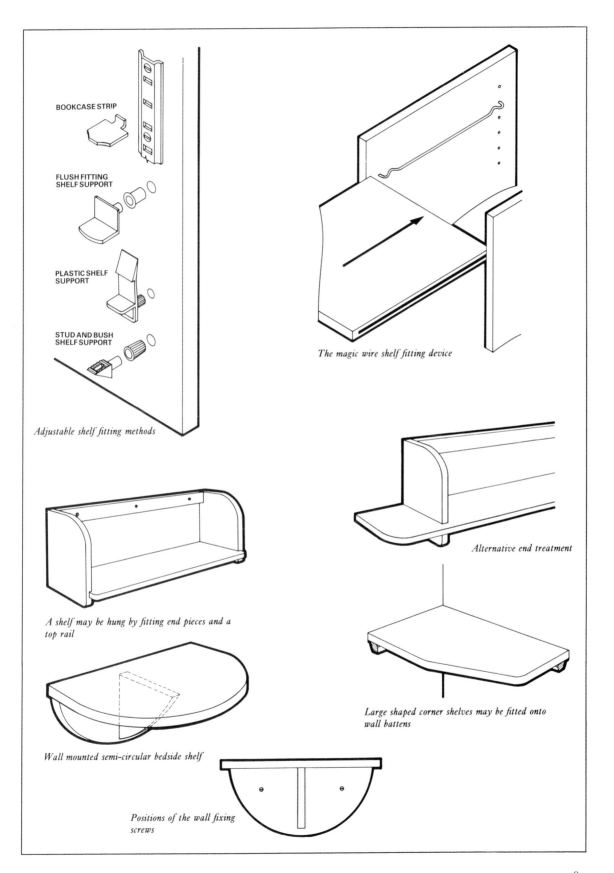

BOOKCASE STRIP

FLUSH FITTING
SHELF SUPPORT

PLASTIC SHELF
SUPPORT

STUD AND BUSH
SHELF SUPPORT

Adjustable shelf fitting methods

The magic wire shelf fitting device

A shelf may be hung by fitting end pieces and a top rail

Alternative end treatment

Wall mounted semi-circular bedside shelf

Large shaped corner shelves may be fitted onto wall battens

Positions of the wall fixing screws

23 Storage

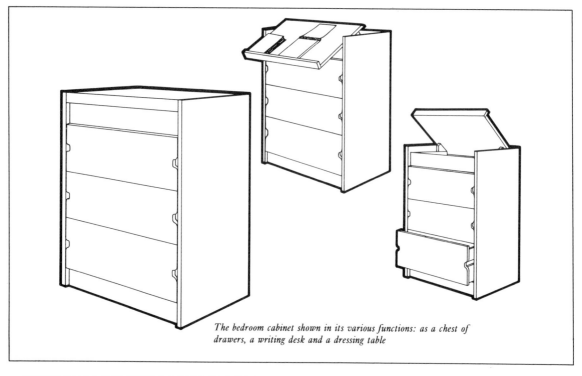

The bedroom cabinet shown in its various functions: as a chest of drawers, a writing desk and a dressing table

BEDROOM CABINET / WORK DESK / DRESSING TABLE
(Overall dimensions: 680 × 457 × 854mm high; 26¾ × 18 × 33¾ in)

The main feature of this bedroom cabinet is the lid which can be lifted up to reveal a shallow tray or pulled forward to become a comfortable working surface. The tray may be used to store writing equipment and books or, if the cabinet is being used as a dressing table, cosmetics might be kept there. In the latter case a mirror might be fitted to the underside of the lid, but the top of the front rail will have to be adapted as explained later. The movement of the lid is controlled by dowels which run in channels in a pair of guide plates which are mounted inside the cabinet. When the top is used in the forward position plenty of leg room is created and the handles of the drawers are in the form of cut-outs so that this space is uninterrupted. The lip on the leading edge of the cabinet lid serves to hold books or equipment on the surface. Full details of the cabinet construction are given in the orthographic drawing.

The main construction of the cabinet consists of two side panels spaced apart by four rails. The top and bottom back rails are fitted flush with the back edge of the side panels whilst the front rails are set back by 16mm (⅝in). The top front rail has a shaped solid wood strip fitted to it and is also positioned 32mm (1¼in) down from the top of the side panels. (It is this solid wood strip that should be replaced by short blocks fitted at either end of the rail if a mirror is fitted so that the sliding motion of the lid is not affected.) All four rails should be securely fitted with a chosen type of K.D. fitting as these form the basic frame of the cabinet. The shallow tray which fits just underneath the lid is constructed as a separate unit with lap joints, the base being glued and pinned onto the bottom. This tray is finally fitted into the cabinet by screwing through into the top back and front rails from inside the tray, but this will be one of the final operations to be carried out. The back panel of the cabinet is fitted onto mounting strips which are pinned or screwed onto the backs of the two back rails and also down the insides of the side panels.

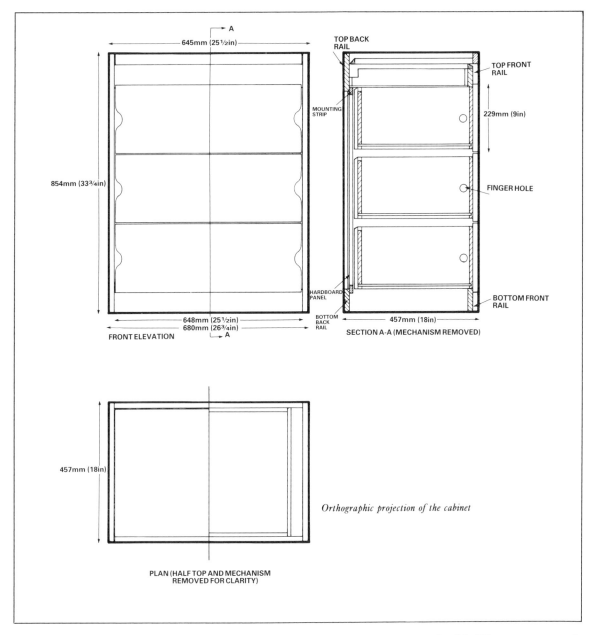

645mm (25½in)

TOP BACK RAIL

TOP FRONT RAIL

MOUNTING STRIP

229mm (9in)

854mm (33¾in)

FINGER HOLE

HARDBOARD PANEL

BOTTOM BACK RAIL

648mm (25½in)
680mm (26¾in)

BOTTOM FRONT RAIL

457mm (18in)

FRONT ELEVATION

SECTION A-A (MECHANISM REMOVED)

457mm (18in)

Orthographic projection of the cabinet

PLAN (HALF TOP AND MECHANISM REMOVED FOR CLARITY)

The lid consists of a panel of veneered or melamine-faced chipboard with a solid wood edging strip at the back and a deep solid wood lip at the front. The strip at the back is glued onto the chipboard edge and shaped so that it clears the back rail when the lid is raised to rest just over the vertical. The front lip should perhaps be dowel-jointed or fitted with a loose tongue to make it fully secure. Full details of the guide plates and the dowel carrying blocks which are fitted to the lid are given overleaf. The guide plates are made of two layers of 6mm (¼in) birch plywood or acrylic sheet, the inner piece having the channels cut through it. The channels should be carefully marked out and cut with a coping saw or bandsaw, being finished with files to give

a smooth movement on the lid. (If a power router is available it may be used to good effect here.) When completed the guide plates are screwed to the inside of the cabinet in the correct positions and at this point the tray may also be fitted. The blocks which hold the controlling dowels are dowel-jointed to the underside of the lid and when the whole lid assembly is complete it is merely dropped into place and should rest horizontally on top of the guide plates and the top edge of the front rail.

The drawer boxes are constructed with lap joints and the bases are grooved in. The sides of the drawers are grooved to slide on runners which are fitted inside the cabinet with counterbored screws; finger holes are

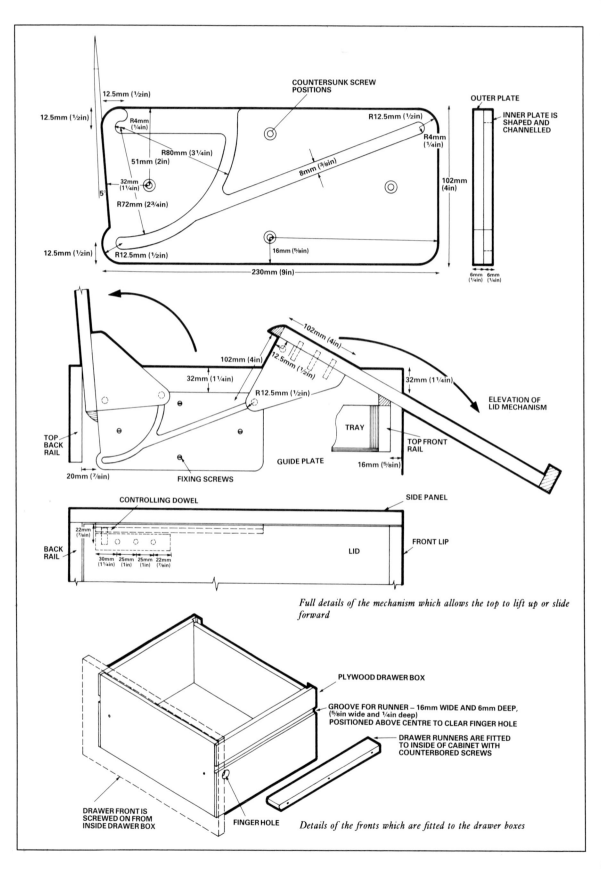

COUNTERSUNK SCREW POSITIONS

12.5mm (½in)

12.5mm (½in)

R4mm (¼in)

R12.5mm (½in)

R4mm (¼in)

OUTER PLATE

INNER PLATE IS SHAPED AND CHANNELLED

R80mm (3¼in)

51mm (2in)

8mm (⅜in)

102mm (4in)

32mm (1¼in)

R72mm (2¾in)

5°

12.5mm (½in)

R12.5mm (½in)

16mm (⅝in)

230mm (9in)

6mm (¼in)   6mm (¼in)

102mm (4in)

12.5mm (½in)

102mm (4in)

32mm (1¼in)

32mm (1¼in)

R12.5mm (½in)

ELEVATION OF LID MECHANISM

TOP BACK RAIL

TRAY

TOP FRONT RAIL

20mm (⅞in)

FIXING SCREWS

GUIDE PLATE

16mm (⅝in)

SIDE PANEL

CONTROLLING DOWEL

22mm (⅞in)

BACK RAIL

LID

FRONT LIP

30mm (1¼in)   25mm (1in)   25mm (1in)   22mm (⅞in)

Full details of the mechanism which allows the top to lift up or slide forward

PLYWOOD DRAWER BOX

GROOVE FOR RUNNER – 16mm WIDE AND 6mm DEEP, (⅝in wide and ¼in deep) POSITIONED ABOVE CENTRE TO CLEAR FINGER HOLE

DRAWER RUNNERS ARE FITTED TO INSIDE OF CABINET WITH COUNTERBORED SCREWS

DRAWER FRONT IS SCREWED ON FROM INSIDE DRAWER BOX

FINGER HOLE

Details of the fronts which are fitted to the drawer boxes

CUTTING LIST

description	material	length	width	thickness	no. off	comments
Side panels	Veneered or melamine-faced chipboard	854mm (33¼in)	457mm (18in)	16mm (⅝in)	2	Edged all round
Top back rail	,,	648mm (25½in)	127mm (5in)	16mm (⅝in)	1	Edged along top edge
Top front rail	,,	648mm (25½in)	76mm (3in)	16mm (⅝in)	1	Width includes a 16mm (⅝in) solid wood strip
Bottom back rail	,,	648mm (25½in)	76mm (3in)	16mm (⅝in)	1	
Bottom front rail	,,	648mm (25½in)	76mm (3in)	16mm (⅝in)	1	
Lid	,,	645mm (25½in)	406mm (16in)	16mm (⅝in)	1	Edged along both sides
Rear edge of lid	Solid wood	645mm (25½in)	16mm (⅝in)	16mm (⅝in)	1	Glued in position
Front lip on lid	,,	645mm (25½in)	32mm (1¼in)	16mm (⅝in)	1	Dowel jointed or loose tongue and groove
Back panel	Hardboard	651mm (25¾in)	647mm (25½in)	3.5mm (⅛in)	1	Pinned onto mounting strips
Mounting strips	Solid wood	648mm (25½in)	25mm (1in)	12mm (½in)	2	Pinned along back rails
Mounting strips	,,	625mm (24½in)	12mm (½in)	12mm (½in)	2	Pinned inside side panels
Tray sides	Plywood	410mm (16¼in)	60mm (2¼in)	12mm (½in)	2	Tray is jointed with lap joints
Tray front	,,	552mm (21¾in)	60mm (2¼in)	12mm (½in)	1	,,
Tray back	,,	552mm (21¾in)	30mm (1¼in)	12mm (½in)	1	,,
Tray base	,,	564mm (22¼in)	410mm (16¼in)	6mm (¼in)	1	Pinned and glued in place
Drawer box sides	Plywood	406mm (16in)	190mm (7½in)	12mm (½in)	6	Drawer boxes are lap jointed
Drawer box fronts	,,	585mm (23in)	190mm (7½in)	12mm (½in)	3	,,
Drawer box backs	,,	585mm (23in)	165mm (6½in)	12mm (½in)	3	Backs are housed into sides
Drawer bases	,,	573mm (22½in)	400mm (15¾in)	6mm (¼in)	3	Bases are grooved in
Drawer fronts	Veneered or melamine-faced chipboard	645mm (25½in)	229mm (9in)	16mm (⅝in)	3	Edged all round. Handle cut-outs at both ends
Drawer runners	Hardwood	406mm (16in)	32mm (1¼in)	16mm (⅝in)	6	Fitted inside cabinet with counterbored screws
Guide plates	Birch plywood or acrylic sheet	230mm (9in)	102mm (4in)	6mm (¼in)	4	The two inner plates are channelled to accept 8mm dowels
Dowel carrying blocks on lid	Solid wood	102mm (4in)	102mm (4in)	21mm (⅞in)	1	Dowelled onto underside of lid
Controlling dowels	Dowel rod	25mm (1in)	8mm (⅜in) diameter		4	

drilled through the drawer sides directly behind the cut-outs in the drawer fronts. These cut-outs are shaped so that iron-on edging strip can be applied with the toe of the iron and consequently a smooth, rounded shape must be achieved. The drawer fronts are fitted to the drawers by screwing through from the inside.

Relevant techniques and chapter nos.
Dowel joints (3)
Lap joints (4)
Loose tongue and groove joint (9)
Edging manufactured board (11)
K.D. fittings (12)
Drawer construction (14)

ISLAND UNIT
(Overall dimensions: 900 × 900 × 510mm high; 35½ × 35½ × 20in)

The island unit is an attractive centrepiece for a room and serves as a coffee or supper table as well as being a useful storage area for records, magazines, bottles, glasses and any other items which may normally cause clutter. The unit may be mounted on castors with plate fixings if mobility is required and the use of melamine-faced chipboard for the shelving and partitions makes the unit easy to wipe clean. Details of the construction and dimensions of the unit are shown in the diagrams.

Due to their size, the top and baseboard must be cut from a 2440 × 1220mm (96 × 48in) sheet of veneered chipboard or, alternatively, made by glueing laminate onto 15mm (⅝in) plain chipboard. The corners of the top and base are rounded at a radius of 10mm (⅜in) and the

boards are edged all round with strips of plastic laminate or with iron-on edging strip. If a plastic tub is to be let into the top to hold a plant, an accurate hole should be cut in the centre of the top so that the tub will rest on its lip when lowered in. The maximum size for the tub hole is 180mm (7⅛in) square.

The four main partitions and the sides to the drawer compartment and the drinks cupboard should all have any outward-facing edges covered with strips of plastic laminate or iron-on edging and may be fitted with dowels into the top and base boards or jointed with discreet K.D. fittings. The two shelves are dowel-jointed into the partitions and it will be found that the whole partition structure must be asembled with the shelves in position before the top and bottom boards are fitted on. The drilling of the holes for the record storage rods and the fixing of the shelf supporting pillar

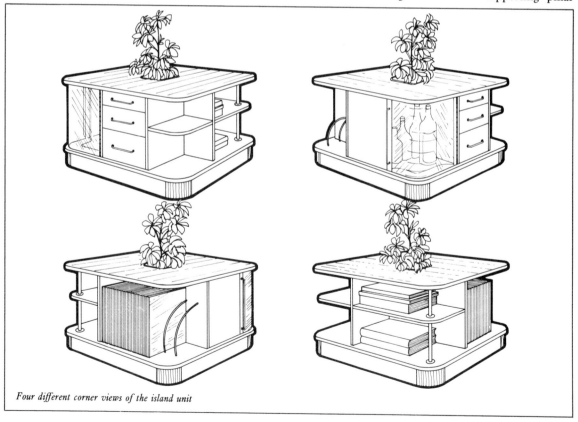

Four different corner views of the island unit

94

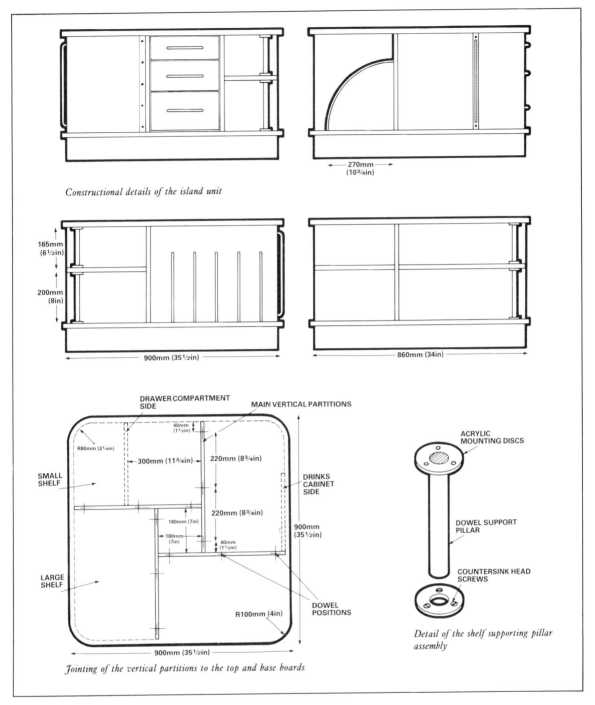

Constructional details of the island unit

165mm
(6½in)

200mm
(8in)

900mm (35½in)

860mm (34in)

DRAWER COMPARTMENT
SIDE

MAIN VERTICAL PARTITIONS

40mm
(1½in)

R80mm (3¼in)

300mm (11¾in)

220mm (8¾in)

SMALL
SHELF

DRINKS
CABINET
SIDE

220mm (8¾in)

180mm (7in)

180mm
(7in)

40mm
(1½in)

900mm
(35½in)

LARGE
SHELF

R100mm (4in)

DOWEL
POSITIONS

900mm (35½in)

270mm
(10¾in)

ACRYLIC
MOUNTING DISCS

DOWEL SUPPORT
PILLAR

COUNTERSINK HEAD
SCREWS

Detail of the shelf supporting pillar
assembly

Jointing of the vertical partitions to the top and base boards

mounting discs should also be carried out before the main body of the unit is assembled.

The plinth consists of four lengths of veneered chipboard glued to shaped softwood corner blocks which provide the rounded corners required to match the overall design. These joints should be strengthened by nailing and glueing support blocks at the back. Plastic modesty blocks or wooden blocks are used to screw the plinth in position under the base board and

the softwood corner blocks can be dyed or painted to contrast or match with the plinth side material.

The drawers are, essentially, plywood boxes to which a base is glued and pinned and a drawer front screwed. The boxes are constructed with lap joints which are pinned and glued and the drawer front is secured by screwing from inside the drawer. The positioning of the drawer fronts is critical and is as follows: the top drawer front is fitted flush with the top of the drawer box, the

95

CUTTING LIST

description	material	length	width	thickness	no. off	comments
Top and baseboard	Veneered chipboard	900mm ($35\frac{1}{2}$in)	900mm ($35\frac{1}{2}$in)	18mm ($\frac{3}{4}$in)	2	Edged all round with iron-on edging strip or laminate strip
Main vertical partitions	Melamine-faced chipboard	520mm ($20\frac{1}{2}$in)	381mm (15in)	16mm ($\frac{5}{8}$in)	4	Outward-facing edges must be covered with edging strip
Side to drawer compartment	,,	325mm ($12\frac{3}{4}$in)	381mm (15in)	16mm ($\frac{5}{8}$in)	1	,,
Side to drinks cabinet	,,	310mm ($12\frac{1}{4}$in)	381mm (15in)	16mm ($\frac{5}{8}$in)	1	,,
Large shelf	,,	520mm ($20\frac{1}{2}$in)	325mm ($12\frac{3}{4}$in)	16mm ($\frac{5}{8}$in)	1	,,
Small shelf	,,	325mm ($12\frac{3}{4}$in)	204mm (8in)	16mm ($\frac{5}{8}$in)	1	,,
Plinth sides	Veneered chipboard	710mm (28in)	90mm ($3\frac{1}{2}$in)	18mm ($\frac{3}{4}$in)	4	
Plinth corner blocks	Softwood	90mm ($3\frac{1}{2}$in)	110mm ($4\frac{1}{4}$in)	50mm (2in)	4	The corner blocks are shaped and jointed to the plinth sides
Drawer fronts	Melamine-faced chipboard					The drawer fronts are screwed to the drawer boxes
Top	,,	297mm ($11\frac{3}{4}$in)	95mm ($3\frac{3}{4}$in)	16mm ($\frac{5}{8}$in)	1	
Middle	,,	297mm ($11\frac{3}{4}$in)	125mm (5in)	16mm ($\frac{5}{8}$in)	1	
Bottom	,,	297mm ($11\frac{3}{4}$in)	155mm (6in)	16mm ($\frac{5}{8}$in)	1	
Drawer sides	Plywood					
Top	,,	300mm ($11\frac{3}{4}$in)	80mm ($3\frac{1}{4}$in)	12mm ($\frac{1}{2}$in)	2	
Middle	,,	300mm ($11\frac{3}{4}$in)	85mm ($3\frac{1}{4}$in)	12mm ($\frac{1}{2}$in)	2	
Bottom	,,	300mm ($11\frac{3}{4}$in)	140mm ($5\frac{1}{2}$in)	12mm ($\frac{1}{2}$in)	2	
Drawer box fronts	Plywood					
Top	,,	297mm ($11\frac{3}{4}$in)	80mm ($3\frac{1}{4}$in)	12mm ($\frac{1}{2}$in)	1	
Middle	,,	297mm ($11\frac{3}{4}$in)	85mm ($3\frac{1}{4}$in)	12mm ($\frac{1}{2}$in)	1	
Bottom	,,	297mm ($11\frac{3}{4}$in)	140mm ($5\frac{1}{2}$in)	12mm ($\frac{1}{2}$in)	1	
Drawer box backs	Plywood					
Top	,,	285mm ($11\frac{1}{4}$in)	80mm ($3\frac{1}{4}$in)	12mm ($\frac{1}{2}$in)	1	
Middle	,,	285mm ($11\frac{1}{4}$in)	85mm ($3\frac{1}{4}$in)	12mm ($\frac{1}{2}$in)	1	
Bottom	,,	285mm ($11\frac{1}{4}$in)	140mm ($5\frac{1}{2}$in)	12mm ($\frac{1}{2}$in)	1	
Drawer bases	Plywood	306mm (12in)	297mm ($11\frac{3}{4}$in)	6mm ($\frac{1}{4}$in)	3	The drawer bases are pinned and glued in position
Drawer runners	Hardwood	309mm ($12\frac{1}{4}$in)	22mm ($\frac{7}{8}$in)	12mm ($\frac{1}{2}$in)	4	
Bottom drawer running strips	Plastic laminate	309mm ($12\frac{1}{4}$in)	12mm ($\frac{1}{2}$in)	1.5mm ($\frac{1}{16}$in)	2	
Dowel pillar	Dowel rod	165mm ($6\frac{1}{2}$in)	19mm ($\frac{3}{4}$in) diameter		1	Dowel pillars are dyed or painted
,,	,,	200mm ($7\frac{3}{4}$in)	19mm ($\frac{3}{4}$in) diameter		1	
Mounting discs	Acrylic sheet	45mm ($1\frac{3}{4}$in) diameter		3.5mm ($\frac{1}{8}$in)	4	The mounting discs are screwed in position
Corner blocks for plinth joints	Softwood	90mm ($3\frac{1}{2}$in)	15mm ($\frac{5}{8}$in)	15mm ($\frac{5}{8}$in)	8	
Drinks cabinet door supports	Acrylic sheet	325mm ($12\frac{3}{4}$in)	210mm ($8\frac{1}{4}$in)	4mm ($\frac{1}{4}$in)	2	The supports are shaped and glued to the door itself

description	material	length	width	thickness	no. off	comments
Door material	,,	500mm (19¾in)	370mm (14½in)	4mm (¼in)	1	The door shape is heat-formed
Door corner supports	Hardwood	370mm (14½in)	20mm (¾in)	15mm (⅝in)	2	These supports allow the hinge and catches to be fitted

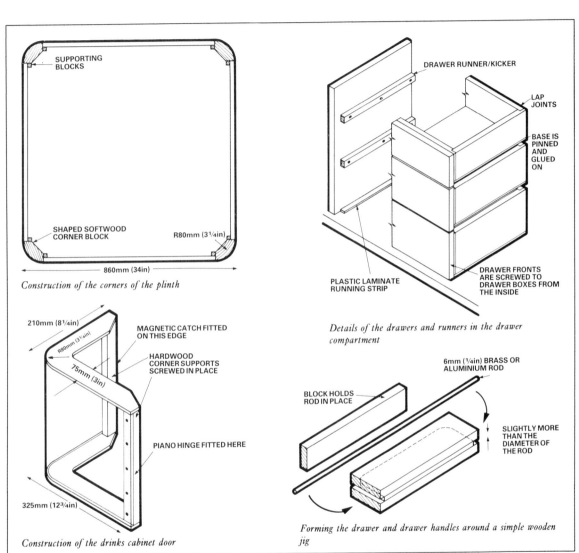

Construction of the corners of the plinth

Details of the drawers and runners in the drawer compartment

Construction of the drinks cabinet door

Forming the drawer and drawer handles around a simple wooden jig

middle drawer front is fitted leaving a 10mm (⅜in) overlap both above and below the box, and the bottom drawer front is fitted with a 10mm (⅜in) overlap above the drawer box. (This system allows the drawer runners to double as kickers when they are screwed to the inside rails of the drawer compartment.) The plastic laminate strips are glued to the baseboard to allow the bottom drawer to run smoothly without scraping across the baseboard.

The door to the drinks cabinet is a construction of wood and acrylic sheet and although considerable preparation is required to be able to form the curved door, the end result justifies this effort. Once the clear acrylic has been formed the two hardwood support strips are screwed into place with small countersink head screws. The two shaped acrylic supports, which may be coloured, are then fixed on the top and bottom of the door with the appropriate adhesive, then trimmed flush. The door is best hung on a length of piano hinge and should be fitted with a magnetic catch.

The handles and record storage rods on the unit can be made from 6mm (¼in) metal rod. Brass or aluminium rod can easily be formed around a wooden jig and, when trimmed to length, is glued into blind holes drilled into the drawer fronts and the drinks cabinet door.

Relevant techniques and chapter nos.
Dowel joints (3)
K.D. joints and fittings (12)
Drawer construction (17)
Castors and catches (18)
Working acrylic sheet (20)

MULTI-PURPOSE STORAGE UNITS
(Overall dimensions: 610 × 457 × 726mm high; 24 × 18 × 28½in)

The design presented here is for a storage unit which can be adapted to serve any one of a variety of storage needs. The basic unit can be made in either a wide and shallow or narrow and deep format, the construction method being the same in both cases. The units may be self-contained, free-standing items of furniture, with or without castors, or they may be used as supports for a desk top or working surface.

The material best suited for making the units is veneered or melamine-faced chipboard and the boards which go together to form each unit can be jointed with dowels or K.D. fittings. If the back panel is not to be seen the veneered or melamine-faced chipboard may be substituted with hardboard or plywood, a rebate being formed by fitting supporting strips onto the inside faces of the side panels and the base being lengthened to make up the difference between 16mm ($\frac{5}{8}$in) chipboard and the thinner hardboard or plywood. If the unit is to be free-standing the top is laid over the base of the unit, overlapping by 5mm ($\frac{3}{16}$in) all round. The top panel itself may be edged with iron-on edging strip or solid wood lipping and must be cut to size accordingly.

If the unit is to be a support for a desk top or working surface the top panel will be inset into the cabinet and the working surface attached by screwing up through the top of the base unit. The desk top or working surface would be made of blockboard and this can be edged with a deep solid wood lipping which will help to locate the top on the base units. A veneered blockboard would

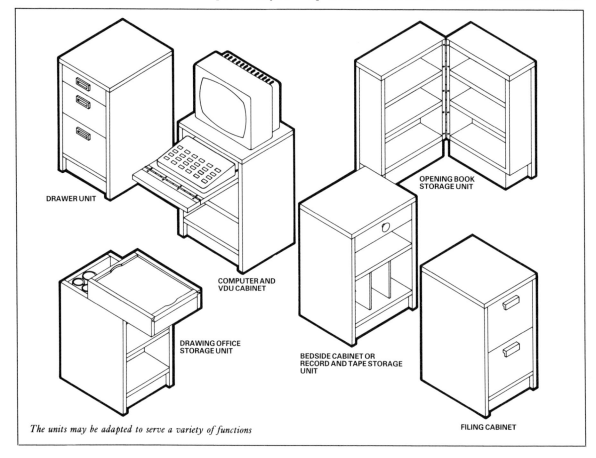

DRAWER UNIT

COMPUTER AND VDU CABINET

DRAWING OFFICE STORAGE UNIT

OPENING BOOK STORAGE UNIT

BEDSIDE CABINET OR RECORD AND TAPE STORAGE UNIT

FILING CABINET

The units may be adapted to serve a variety of functions

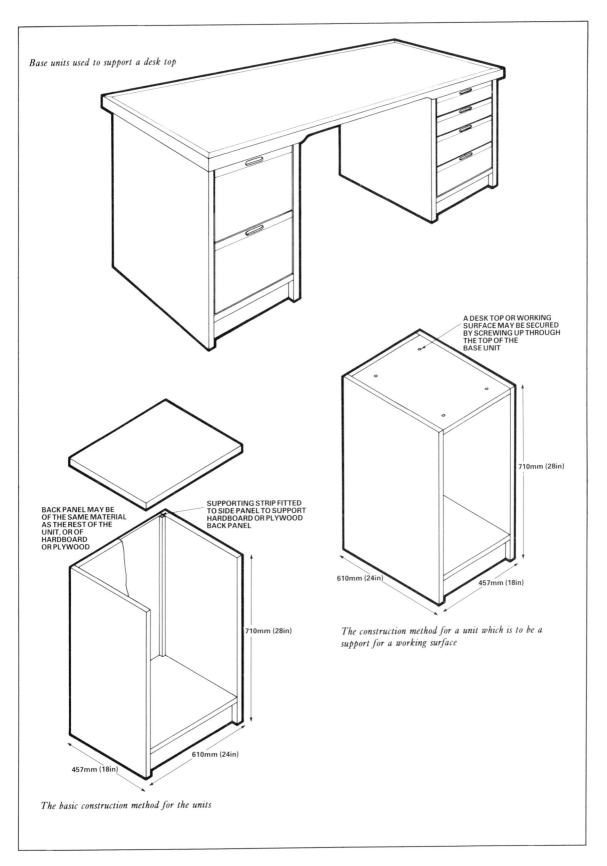

Base units used to support a desk top

A DESK TOP OR WORKING
SURFACE MAY BE SECURED
BY SCREWING UP THROUGH
THE TOP OF THE
BASE UNIT

710mm (28in)

610mm (24in)

457mm (18in)

The construction method for a unit which is to be a support for a working surface

BACK PANEL MAY BE
OF THE SAME MATERIAL
AS THE REST OF THE
UNIT, OR OF
HARDBOARD
OR PLYWOOD

SUPPORTING STRIP FITTED
TO SIDE PANEL TO SUPPORT
HARDBOARD OR PLYWOOD
BACK PANEL

710mm (28in)

610mm (24in)

457mm (18in)

The basic construction method for the units

make a very attractive desk top but some working conditions would be better served by plain blockboard covered with a sheet of plastic laminate.

There are further options which are open when the units are to be used in conjunction with a desk top or working surface. Rather than using two units to support a surface, one at either end, one end of the surface may be supported by an end frame or by resting on a batten fixed to the wall. In such a situation a mobile unit on castors may be accommodated under the working surface to be used both at the desk and also elsewhere in the room.

Relevant techniques and chapter nos.

Dowel joints (3)
Edging manufactured board (11)
K.D. fittings (12)
Drawer construction (17)
Castors (18)

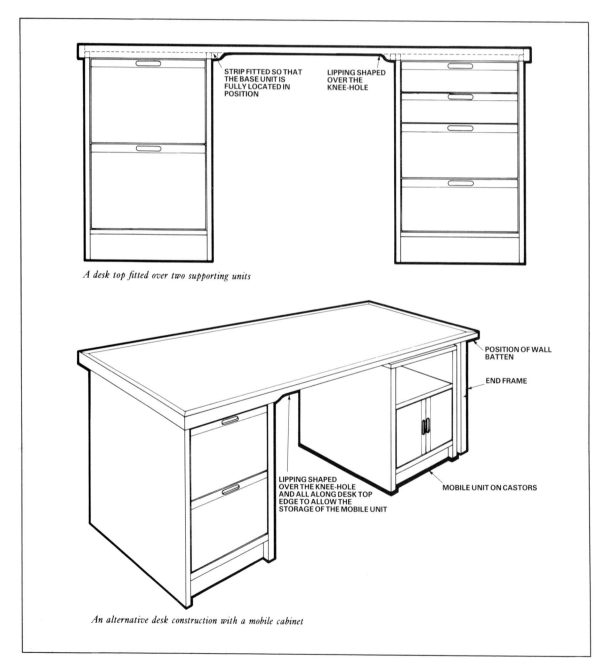

A desk top fitted over two supporting units

STRIP FITTED SO THAT THE BASE UNIT IS FULLY LOCATED IN POSITION

LIPPING SHAPED OVER THE KNEE-HOLE

POSITION OF WALL BATTEN

END FRAME

MOBILE UNIT ON CASTORS

LIPPING SHAPED OVER THE KNEE-HOLE AND ALL ALONG DESK TOP EDGE TO ALLOW THE STORAGE OF THE MOBILE UNIT

An alternative desk construction with a mobile cabinet

description	material	length	width	thickness	no. off	comments
Deep unit						
Side panels	Veneered or melamine-faced chipboard	710mm (28in)	610mm (24in)	16mm ($\frac{5}{8}$in)	2	Edging strip applied to bottom edge
Back panel	,,	425mm ($16\frac{3}{4}$in)	710mm (28in)	16mm ($\frac{5}{8}$in)	1	,,
Base	,,	594mm ($24\frac{1}{2}$in)	425mm ($16\frac{3}{4}$in)	16mm ($\frac{5}{8}$in)	1	Edging strip on front edge
Kickboard	,,	425mm ($16\frac{3}{4}$in)	80mm ($3\frac{1}{4}$in)	16mm ($\frac{5}{8}$in)	1	
Inset top	,,	610mm (24in)	457mm (18in)	16mm ($\frac{5}{8}$in)	1	Edging strip on front edge
Lay-on top	,,	620mm ($24\frac{1}{2}$in)	467mm ($18\frac{1}{2}$in)	16mm ($\frac{5}{8}$in)	1	Edged all round with iron-on strip or solid wood lipping
Wide unit						
Side panels	Veneered or melamine-faced chipboard	710mm (28in)	457mm (18in)	16mm ($\frac{5}{8}$in)	2	Edging strip applied to bottom edge
Back panel	,,	710mm (28in)	578mm ($22\frac{3}{4}$in)	16mm ($\frac{5}{8}$in)	1	,,
Base	,,	578mm ($22\frac{3}{4}$in)	441mm ($17\frac{1}{4}$in)	16mm ($\frac{5}{8}$in)	1	Edging strip on front edge
Kickboard	,,	578mm ($22\frac{3}{4}$in)	80mm ($3\frac{1}{4}$in)	16mm ($\frac{5}{8}$in)	1	
Inset top	,,	578mm ($22\frac{3}{4}$in)	441mm ($17\frac{1}{4}$in)	16mm ($\frac{5}{8}$in)	1	Edging strip on front edge
Lay-on top	,,	620mm ($24\frac{1}{2}$in)	467mm ($18\frac{1}{2}$in)	16mm ($\frac{5}{8}$in)	1	Edged all round with iron-on strip or solid wood lipping

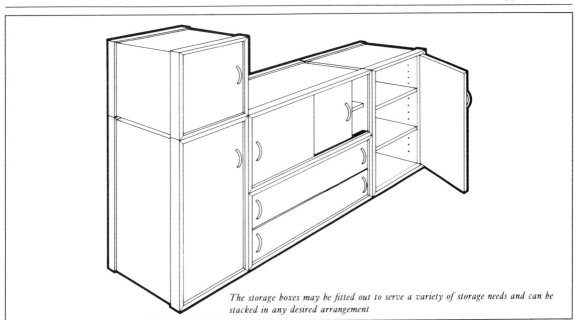

The storage boxes may be fitted out to serve a variety of storage needs and can be stacked in any desired arrangement

STACKING STORAGE BOXES

This storage system has been designed to be extremely versatile and consists of two basic units: a square box, and a rectangular box with side lengths in the ratio of 2:1. Each box may be fitted out to solve a particular storage problem and as a consequence may have a hinged wooden or glass door, shelves, sliding doors, and drawers or may be left as a simple open box in which items are displayed.

The boxes are made of veneered or melamine-faced chipboard and are constructed using a pair of K.D. fittings along each corner joint, the fittings preferably being of a type which lie flush with the board surface, so as not to intrude into the internal space of the box. The appearance of the basic boxes is enhanced by the application of solid wood trim of a matching or contrasting colour to the board material to both the front and rear edges. The trim is mitred at the corners and is pinned around the back edge of the box so that it forms a rebate into which the back panel of hardboard can be fitted. The trim at the front may be made by rebating a 32 × 22mm ($1\frac{1}{4} \times \frac{7}{8}$in) solid wood section or it may be fabricated by joining separate 32 × 6mm ($1\frac{1}{4} \times \frac{1}{4}$in) and 16 × 16mm ($\frac{5}{8} \times \frac{5}{8}$in) sections together. The front edge of this trim may be chamfered or rounded to further improve the appearance of the boxes.

If partitions are to be fitted into the boxes they may be dowelled into position or fitted into housings. Through housings can be used as the front trim will cover the joint when it is fitted.

It is the weight of each unit which keeps it in position on top of another and all that is required is a locating device to prevent any movement if the boxes are accidentally knocked. The simplest method of providing this location is to fit loose lengths of 6 or 8mm ($\frac{1}{4}$ or $\frac{5}{16}$in) dowel into blind holes drilled into the boxes along the trim. On the square boxes these holes should be exactly halfway along the sides and indeed this is also the case on the short sides of the rectangular box. Along the long side of the rectangular box the centres for these holes will be at a distance of a quarter of the side length from both ends (fig. 389). It is recommended that these holes should only be drilled as they become necessary for any particular arrangement of the storage boxes.

Relevant techniques and chapter nos.

Housing joints (7)
K.D. fittings (12)
Drawer construction (17)
Sliding door channel (18)
Adjustable and fixed shelving (22)

CUTTING LIST

description	material	length	width	thickness	no. off	comments
Small unit						
Side panels	Veneered or melamine-faced chipboard	391mm ($15\frac{1}{2}$in)	381mm ($15\frac{1}{2}$in)	16mm ($\frac{5}{8}$in)	2	Edging strip is applied to top and bottom edges
Top and base panels	,,	381mm (15in)	359mm ($14\frac{1}{4}$in)	16mm ($\frac{5}{8}$in)	2	
Rear trim	Solid wood	403mm ($15\frac{3}{4}$in)	32mm ($1\frac{1}{4}$in)	6mm ($\frac{1}{4}$in)	4	Jointed with mitres at the corners and pinned into place
Front trim	,,	403mm ($15\frac{3}{4}$in)	32mm ($1\frac{1}{4}$in)	22mm ($\frac{7}{8}$in)	4	Rebated or made up of 32 × 6mm ($1\frac{1}{4} \times \frac{1}{4}$in) and 16 × 16mm ($\frac{5}{8} \times \frac{5}{8}$in) sections glued together
Back panel	Hardboard	391mm ($15\frac{1}{2}$in)	391mm ($15\frac{1}{2}$in)	3.5mm ($\frac{1}{8}$in)	1	Pinned into position
Large unit						
Side panels	Veneered or melamine-faced chipboard	794mm ($31\frac{1}{4}$in)	381mm (15in)	16mm ($\frac{5}{8}$in)	2	Edging strip is applied to top and bottom edges
Top and base panels	,,	381mm (15in)	359mm ($14\frac{1}{4}$in)	16mm ($\frac{5}{8}$in)	2	
Rear trim	Solid wood	806mm ($31\frac{3}{4}$in)	32mm ($1\frac{1}{4}$in)	6mm ($\frac{1}{4}$in)	2	Jointed with mitres at the corners and pinned into place
,,	,,	403mm ($15\frac{3}{4}$in)	32mm ($1\frac{1}{4}$in)	6mm ($\frac{1}{4}$in)	2	
Front trim	,,	806mm ($31\frac{3}{4}$in)	32mm ($1\frac{1}{4}$in)	22mm ($\frac{7}{8}$in)	2	Rebated or made up of 32 × 6mm ($1\frac{1}{4} \times \frac{1}{4}$in) and 16 × 16mm ($\frac{5}{8} \times \frac{5}{8}$in) sections glued together
,,	,,	403mm ($15\frac{3}{4}$in)	32mm ($1\frac{1}{4}$in)	22mm ($\frac{7}{8}$in)	2	
Back panel	Hardboard	794mm ($31\frac{1}{4}$in)	391mm ($15\frac{1}{2}$in)	3.5mm ($\frac{1}{8}$in)	1	Pinned into position

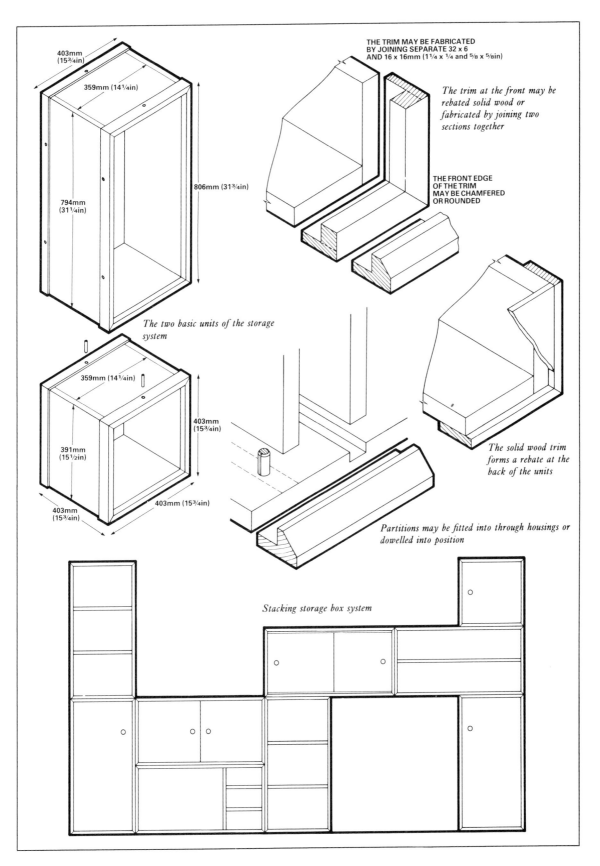

403mm (15¾in)

359mm (14¼in)

806mm (31¾in)

794mm (31¼in)

The two basic units of the storage system

THE TRIM MAY BE FABRICATED BY JOINING SEPARATE 32 x 6 AND 16 x 16mm (1¼ x ¼ and ⅝ x ⅝in)

The trim at the front may be rebated solid wood or fabricated by joining two sections together

THE FRONT EDGE OF THE TRIM MAY BE CHAMFERED OR ROUNDED

359mm (14¼in)

403mm (15¾in)

391mm (15½in)

403mm (15¾in)

403mm (15¾in)

The solid wood trim forms a rebate at the back of the units

Partitions may be fitted into through housings or dowelled into position

Stacking storage box system

103

24 Seating

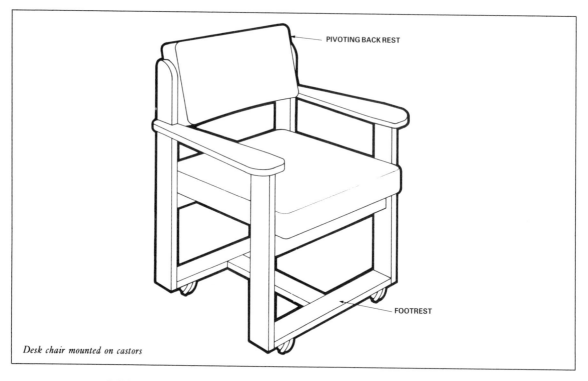

PIVOTING BACK REST

FOOTREST

Desk chair mounted on castors

DESK CHAIR
**(Overall dimensions: 570 × 450 × 820mm
high; $22\frac{1}{2}$ × $17\frac{3}{4}$ × $32\frac{1}{4}$in)**

The construction of this chair is relatively simple but the result is a comfortable seat which would be used at a desk or working surface. The chair may be mounted on castors for mobility or the legs may be extended to make a static chair. This option is shown in the orthographic drawing.

The construction method consists of flat rails jointed across the bottom of each pair of legs, and vertical rails set at a suitable height across each pair of legs to support the seat platform. There are a number of alternative jointing methods which may be used to construct these frames and the method chosen will depend upon the facilities available. The lower joints may be finger or dowel joints, but perhaps an easier and stronger joint would be achieved by screwing into fixing plugs or a dowel set into the ends of the rails. The screws would be slightly counterbored and the heads covered with plugs or caps. The joints between the upper rails and the legs

might be dowel or mortise and tenon joints and it should be noted that the length of the rails stated is a shoulder to shoulder measurement, and extra material should be added for certain jointing methods, e.g. the mortise and tenon joint. The same applies to the central rail which is jointed between the front and the back lower rails.

The arms of the chair are shaped and fitted to the chair frame by making dowel joints between the arms and the front legs and by screwing from the inside faces of the back legs. A shallow housing of 5mm ($\frac{3}{16}$in) depth should be cut into the back legs at the appropriate height to help locate the arms firmly in position. The screw heads may be covered with plugs or caps but this may not be considered necessary as they will be covered by the seat back when it is in position in the chair frame.

The seat of the chair is simply an upholstered panel of 12mm ($\frac{1}{2}$in) plywood secured on top of the upper rails with plastic block fittings, or wooden corner blocks, set inside the rails. The back of the chair is designed to rotate so that it will take up the required position at any time and, again, basically consists of an upholstered

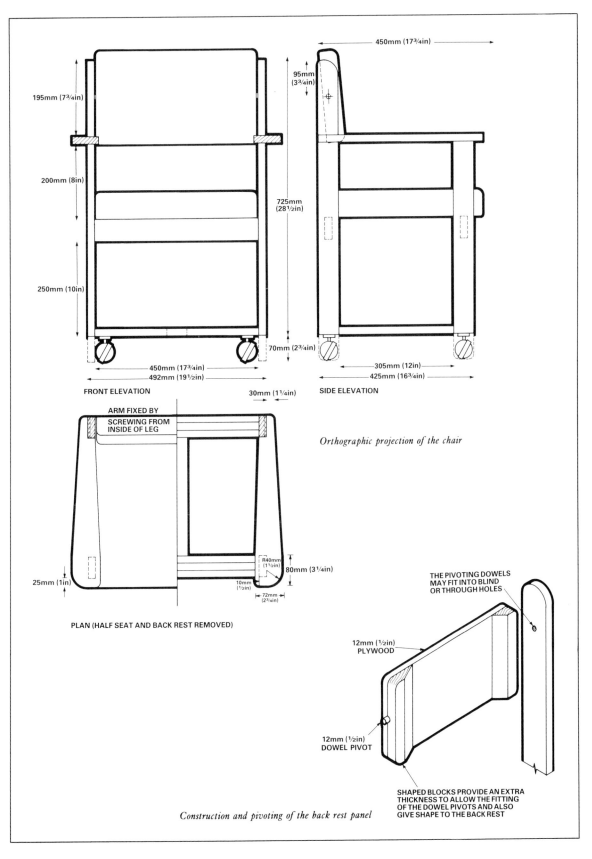

195mm (7¾in)

200mm (8in)

250mm (10in)

725mm (28½in)

450mm (17¾in)
492mm (19½in)

70mm (2¾in)

FRONT ELEVATION

30mm (1¼in)

450mm (17¾in)

95mm (3¾in)

305mm (12in)
425mm (16¾in)

SIDE ELEVATION

ARM FIXED BY SCREWING FROM INSIDE OF LEG

Orthographic projection of the chair

25mm (1in)

R40mm (1½in)

80mm (3¼in)

10mm (½in)

72mm (2¾in)

PLAN (HALF SEAT AND BACK REST REMOVED)

THE PIVOTING DOWELS MAY FIT INTO BLIND OR THROUGH HOLES

12mm (½in) PLYWOOD

12mm (½in) DOWEL PIVOT

SHAPED BLOCKS PROVIDE AN EXTRA THICKNESS TO ALLOW THE FITTING OF THE DOWEL PIVOTS AND ALSO GIVE SHAPE TO THE BACK REST

Construction and pivoting of the back rest panel

panel of 12mm ($\frac{1}{2}$in) plywood. To increase the thickness of the plywood where the pivot is to be fitted, and also to give the back some shape, two shaped wooden blocks are fixed to the panel. The upholstery foam is laid right across the back panel and a curved seat back will result. The back is pivoted on two 12mm dowels which should be set slightly above the middle point of the panel so that the back will always fall into a vertical position when the chair is not in use.

The fully-upholstered back, with the pivoting dowels fitted, may be positioned into blind holes drilled into the inside faces of the back legs when the chair is assembled; or the dowels may be fitted through the legs from the outside where they can be left as a feature or capped in some way.

The lower front rail of the chair is conveniently placed to act as a footrest, but consequently will take a considerable amount of wear; a protective strip of plastic or rubber may be fitted over the front edge of the rail to eliminate this problem.

Relevant techniques and chapter nos.

Dowel joints (3)
Mortise and tenon joints (5)
Housing joints (7)
Screwing preparation and techniques (13)
Upholstery techniques (19)

CUTTING LIST

description	material	length	width	thickness	no. off	comments
Back legs	Softwood or hardwood	725mm (28$\frac{1}{2}$in)	60mm (2$\frac{1}{4}$in)	21mm ($\frac{7}{8}$in)	2	The length stated is for a chair which will be mounted on castors
Front legs	,,	510mm (20in)	60mm (2$\frac{1}{4}$in)	21mm ($\frac{7}{8}$in)	2	,,
Rails	,,	450mm (17$\frac{3}{4}$in)	60mm (2$\frac{1}{4}$in)	21mm ($\frac{7}{8}$in)	4	The lengths given are shoulder to shoulder measurements
Bottom central rail	,,	305mm (12in)	60mm (2$\frac{1}{4}$in)	21mm ($\frac{7}{8}$in)	1	,,
Arms	,,	450mm (17$\frac{3}{4}$in)	72mm (2$\frac{3}{4}$in)	21mm ($\frac{7}{8}$in)	2	The arms are shaped before fitting to the frame
Seat base	Plywood	440mm (17$\frac{1}{4}$in)	430mm (17in)	12mm ($\frac{1}{2}$in)	1	,,
Seat back	,,	440mm (17$\frac{1}{4}$in)	225mm (8$\frac{3}{4}$in)	12mm ($\frac{1}{2}$in)	1	The seat back is pivoted within the chair frame
Shaping blocks	Softwood or hardwood	225mm (8$\frac{3}{4}$in)	21mm ($\frac{7}{8}$in)	60mm (2$\frac{1}{4}$in)	2	These are shaped and glued and pinned to the seat back
Pivots	Dowel rod			12mm ($\frac{1}{2}$in) diameter	2	The length of these pivots will depend on the fitting method used

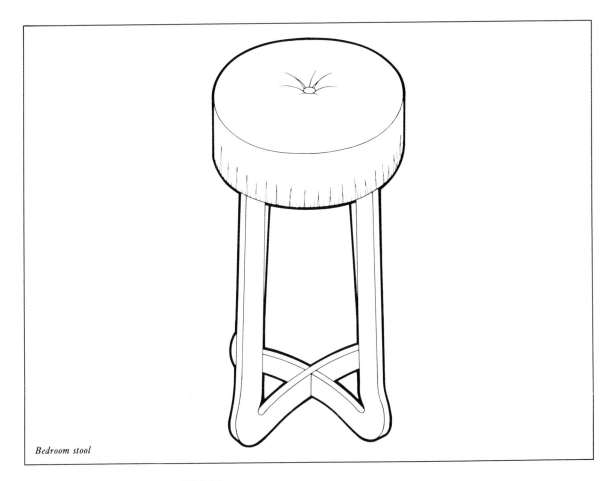

Bedroom stool

BEDROOM STOOL
(Overall dimensions: 400 × 400 × 550mm high; $15\frac{3}{4} \times 15\frac{3}{4} \times 21\frac{1}{2}$in)

The bedroom stool design consists of two matching shaped frames which are jointed at right angles to one another to make a supporting underframe for the seat platform. The seat platform is of 12mm ($\frac{1}{2}$in) plywood and is fixed to the underframe with counterbored screws which pass up through the top rails of the underframe.

The frames are constructed with the material at its full width using dowelled mitre joints at the four corners. The positions and depths of the dowels within the joint must be carefully worked out before the joints are marked out, and this information can only be determined once the design for the final shape of the frames has been decided and drawn full size. To facilitate the drilling of the dowel holes into the 45° angled jointing surfaces at the ends of the frame members, a simple jig can be made to hold the members whilst a pillar drill is used to drill the holes.

To be able to cut the two frames accurately to shape, a template of hardboard or thin plywood should be prepared and pinned to each frame in turn. If hand tools are being used to shape the frame, the coping saw, bow saw or pad saw may play a part in the initial cutting out,

followed by work with spokeshaves or rasps and files to achieve the finished shape. If power tools are available a jig saw might be useful in the early stages but a power router would be extremely helpful as it could be used to cut the shape directly by following the template, given that the machine was fitted with the correct tool.

Once the frames have been shaped the cross-halving joint and the opening at the top of one of the frames can be carried out, and the fixing of the seat platform with counterbored screws through the top rails of the frame can be organised.

The seat platform of 12mm ($\frac{1}{2}$in) plywood will be cut to a shape and size to suit the design of the underframe, but it is most likely to be circular, and will need to be upholstered. The platform itself should have air passage holes drilled through it before the block of foam – which has been cut slightly oversize – is glued in place. A layer of dacron positioned over the foam before the cover is fitted will give the cushion a plump and rounded appearance. The easiest method of covering the foam is to produce a cover of the required material with a draw-string let into the bottom hem. With the cover in place over the foam and platform, the draw-string is pulled tightly and tied under the seat platform. Using this method the cover will be removable for cleaning. A

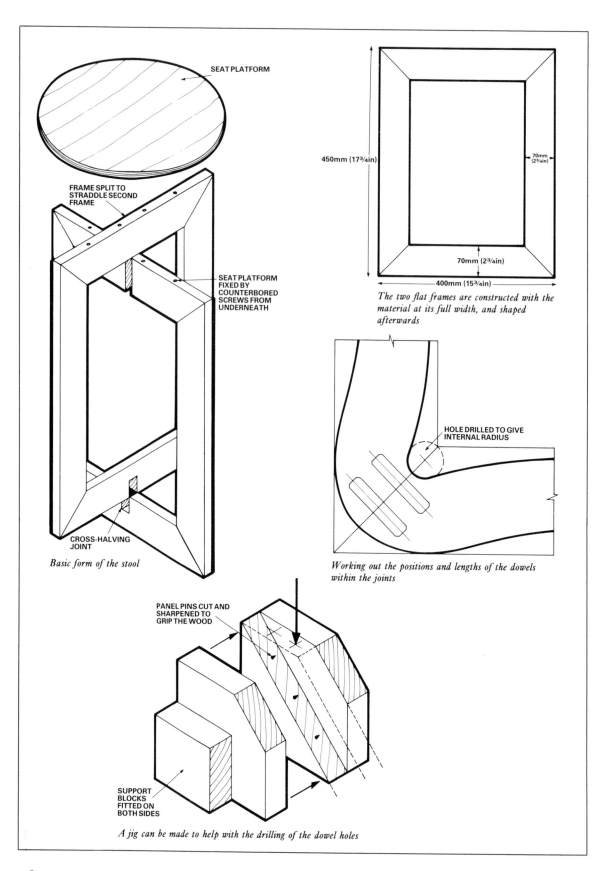

SEAT PLATFORM

FRAME SPLIT TO
STRADDLE SECOND
FRAME

SEAT PLATFORM
FIXED BY
COUNTERBORED
SCREWS FROM
UNDERNEATH

CROSS-HALVING
JOINT

Basic form of the stool

450mm (17¾in)

70mm
(2¾in)

70mm (2¾in)

400mm (15¾in)

*The two flat frames are constructed with the
material at its full width, and shaped
afterwards*

HOLE DRILLED TO GIVE
INTERNAL RADIUS

*Working out the positions and lengths of the dowels
within the joints*

PANEL PINS CUT AND
SHARPENED TO
GRIP THE WOOD

SUPPORT
BLOCKS
FITTED ON
BOTH SIDES

A jig can be made to help with the drilling of the dowel holes

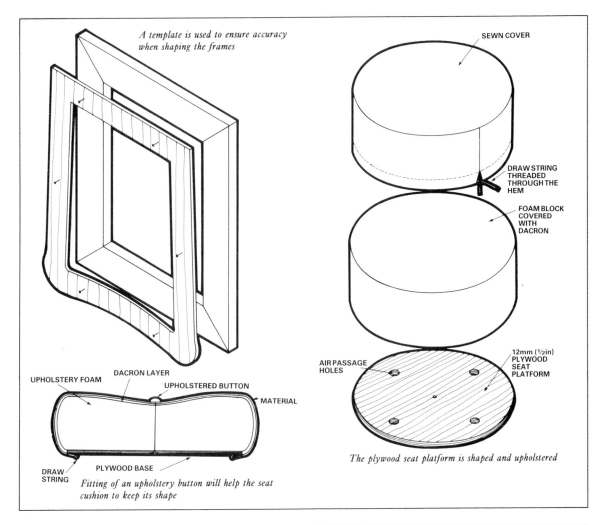

A template is used to ensure accuracy when shaping the frames

SEWN COVER

DRAW STRING THREADED THROUGH THE HEM

FOAM BLOCK COVERED WITH DACRON

12mm (½in) PLYWOOD SEAT PLATFORM

AIR PASSAGE HOLES

The plywood seat platform is shaped and upholstered

UPHOLSTERY FOAM

DACRON LAYER

UPHOLSTERED BUTTON

MATERIAL

DRAW STRING

PLYWOOD BASE

Fitting of an upholstery button will help the seat cushion to keep its shape

further step in upholstering the seat might be the fixing of an upholstery button through the centre of the cushion to help it to keep its shape.

Relevant techniques and chapter nos.

Dowelled joints (3)
Cross-halving joints (4)
Counterboring screws (13)
Upholstery techniques (19)

CUTTING LIST

description	material	length	width	thickness	no. off	comments
Vertical frame members	Hardwood	450mm (17¾in)	70mm (2¾in)	21mm (⅞in)	4	The frames are jointed with dowelled mitres
Horizontal frame members	Hardwood	400mm (15¾in)	70mm (2¾in)	21mm (⅞in)	4	,,
Seat platform	Plywood (12mm; ½in)	The size and shape of the seat platform will depend on the design of the frame			1	The seat platform is fitted by screwing up through the top rails of the underframe

25 Nursery equipment

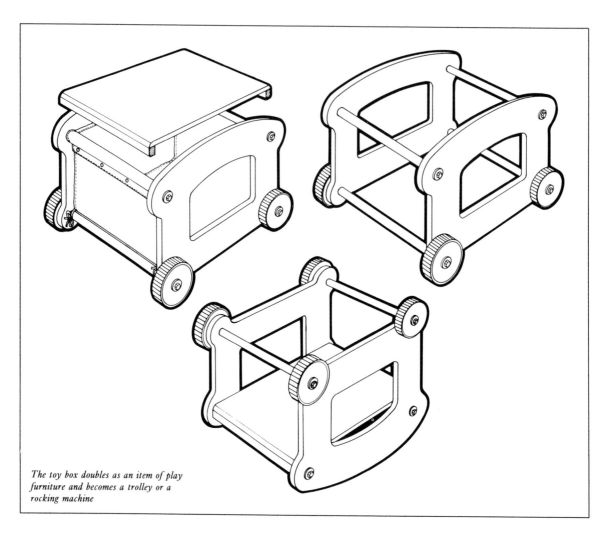

The toy box doubles as an item of play furniture and becomes a trolley or a rocking machine

TOY BOX / PLAY UNIT
(Overall dimensions: 640 × 432 × 500mm high; 25¼ × 17 × 19¾in)

This design for a toy box doubles as an item of play furniture and when the toy-carrying bag has been removed the frame may be used as a trolley or a rocking machine. The construction of the unit is extremely strong and the shapes in the design are rounded for safety.

The two plywood side panels would ideally be made of birch plywood and should be carefully marked out

and cut to shape according to the details on the orthographic drawing. Where each cross rail meets the side panels a 25mm (1in) diameter hole is drilled to a depth of 5mm ($\frac{3}{16}$in) to house the rail, and from the centre of this hole a 6mm ($\frac{1}{4}$in) hole is drilled right through the panel to allow the assembly bolts to pass through. The cross rails are fitted with Scan cross dowels and M6 bolts are used to assemble the unit. (Details of Scan cross dowels can be found in Ch. 12.)

The wheels are made by glueing two 16mm ($\frac{5}{8}$in) plywood discs together, and the four discs which are required to make each pair of wheels can be obtained

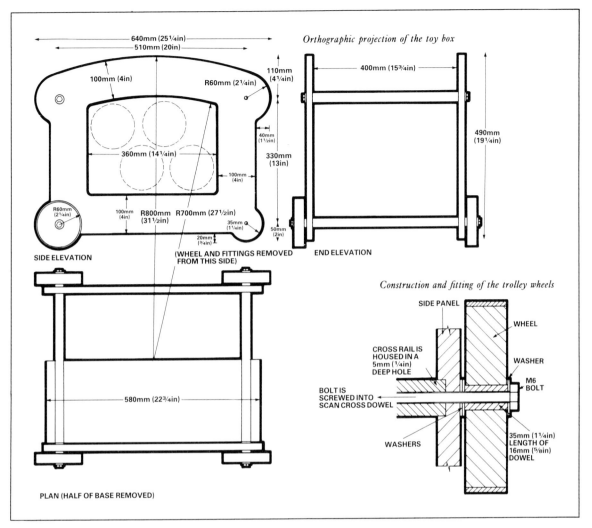

Orthographic projection of the toy box

SIDE ELEVATION

(WHEEL AND FITTINGS REMOVED FROM THIS SIDE)

END ELEVATION

PLAN (HALF OF BASE REMOVED)

Construction and fitting of the trolley wheels

SIDE PANEL

WHEEL

CROSS RAIL IS HOUSED IN A 5mm (¼in) DEEP HOLE

WASHER

M6 BOLT

BOLT IS SCREWED INTO SCAN CROSS DOWEL

WASHERS

35mm (1¼in) LENGTH OF 16mm (⅝in) DOWEL

CUTTING LIST

description	material	length	width	thickness	no. off	comments
Side panels	Plywood	640mm (25¼in)	490mm (19¼in)	16mm (⅝in)	2	The side panels are shaped and pierced
Cross rails	Dowel rod	410mm (16¼in)	25mm (1in) diameter		4	The cross rails are located in shallow holes drilled in the side panels
Wheels	Plywood	120mm (4¾in) diameter		32mm (1¼in)	4	The wheels are made up of two layers of 16mm (⅝in) plywood
Lid/base	Plywood	580mm (22¾in)	396mm (15½in)	16mm (⅝in)	1	
Locating strips	Softwood or hardwood	396mm (15½in)	30mm (1¼in)	20mm (⅞in)	2	The strips are pinned and glued flush with the ends of the lid/base panel
Spacers	Dowel rod	35mm (1¼in)	16mm (⅝in) diameter		4	The spacers are drilled out to allow the assembly bolts to pass through

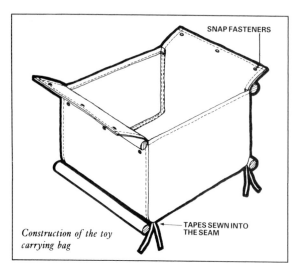

Construction of the toy carrying bag

SNAP FASTENERS

TAPES SEWN INTO THE SEAM

The toy-carrying bag is suspended from the top cross rails and is fastened in place with snap fasteners, consequently the unit can be converted from a toy box to a play unit in seconds and the toys can be left in their container. Once inside the frame the shape of the bag is maintained by tapes which have been sewn into the seams of the bag and which are tied around the lower cross rails.

The lid of the box doubles as the base of the unit when it is being used as a trolley or as a rocking machine. The lid is simply made by pinning and glueing solid wood battens onto a plywood panel, and once the glue has set the top edges of the panel should be rounded for safety.

If birch plywood is used to make the unit, coloured dyes can be used to great effect as the white colour of the plywood will not dull the colour of the dye. A most suitable finish to apply over the dye would be a polyurethane varnish which would be resistant to knocks and would also afford some protection against moisture, should the unit be used outside. The wheels may also be given some protection by fixing rubber belts or strips around them.

from the waste material from the centre of each side panel. A system is required which will allow the bolts to hold the cross rails firmly and yet will also allow the bolts to be used as axles for the wheels – which must turn freely. This is achieved by passing the bolts through a 35mm ($1\frac{3}{8}$in) length of 16mm ($\frac{5}{8}$in) dowel rod with washers fitted at both ends. When tightened the bolts will tighten onto the dowel and hold the cross rails firmly, whilst the wheels which are drilled out to rotate on the dowel will be free to turn; they are held in place by the washers, which must be at least 25mm (1in) in diameter.

Relevant techniques and chapter nos.

Scan cross dowel fittings (12)
Dyes and finishes (14)

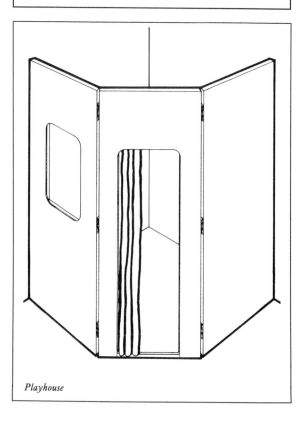

Playhouse

PLAYHOUSE
(Overall folded dimensions:
1220 × 605 × 75mm; 59 × 23¾ × 3in)

The playhouse is designed to be sturdy in use and simple to make. The panels are constructed by fixing hardboard sheets to flat softwood frames and as the panels are joined with screen hinges the playhouse will fold neatly away. The flat softwood frames are constructed with halving joints and the hardboard panels are pinned and glued onto the frames, after any shaping or cutting out has been carried out.

The dimensions given on the drawing are considered to be correct for a playhouse which will be suitable for children up to five years old. There are many ways in which the playhouse may be painted or decorated, and curtains may be hung across the door and window to allow the adult world to be shut out.

Relevant techniques and chapter nos.

Halving joints (4)
Screen hinges (18)

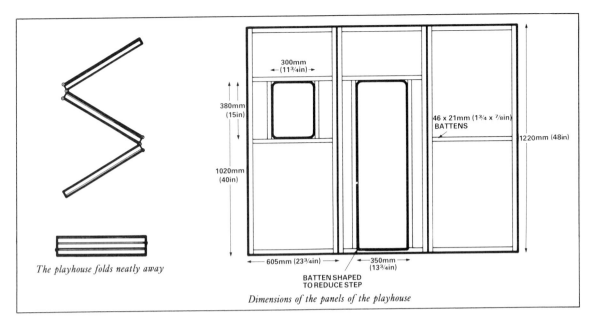

The playhouse folds neatly away

300mm
(11¾in)

380mm
(15in)

46 x 21mm (1¾ x ⁷⁄₈in)
BATTENS

1220mm (48in)

1020mm
(40in)

605mm (23¾in)

350mm
(13¾in)

BATTEN SHAPED
TO REDUCE STEP

Dimensions of the panels of the playhouse

CUTTING LIST

description	material	length	width	thickness	no. off	comments
Panels	Hardboard	1220mm (48in)	605mm (23¾in)	3.5mm (⅛in)	3	Panels are glued and pinned to the softwood frameworks
Frame members	Softwood	16050mm (632¼in)	46mm (1¾in)	21mm (⅞in)		Frameworks are constructed with halving joints

PLAYFRAME
(Overall dimensions: 536 × 460 × 480mm high; 21 × 18 × 19in)

The playframe is designed to hold the interest of babies during the period when they are too young to sit up and yet are wishing to exercise their manipulative skills. A wide variety of objects may be hung from the frame to attract the interest of a child and those shown on the drawings, as examples, are two handle grips of 12mm (½in) dowel, a tennis ball, a small tin containing a wooden ball clapper and a spinning plywood disc, to which are fitted three 8mm (⁵⁄₁₆in) dowel arms capped with wooden balls.

The four legs of the frame are identical and consist of two shaped pieces of 12mm (½in) softwood glued together. Each pair of legs is pivoted at the top by the screw which joins them to the top rail and held apart at the correct distance of about 400mm (15¾in) at the bottom by a loop of string. Fixing plugs are inserted into holes drilled into the ends of the dowel rail to give grip for the screws which are used to fix the leg sections. The rail itself is also glued into a shallow hole drilled for it in the inner leg sections, to prevent rotation. The spinning plywood disc is fitted into the top rail by inserting a length of 12mm (½in) dowel into holes drilled into the

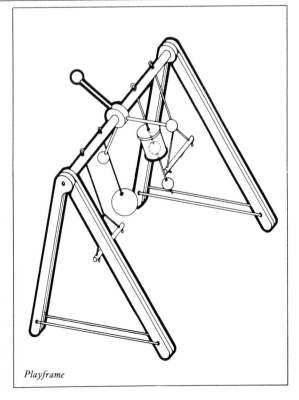

Playframe

ends of the rail where it has been cut in half, the centre of the disc being drilled out to allow it to spin freely on this dowel.

The objects are tied onto the frame using a double thickness of smooth cord or string. The neatest method of attaching the handle grips is shown and a similar method can be used to fix the other objects pictured. The ball is easily hung by forcing a knot through a small hole made in the ball and the tin and wooden ball clapper inside can also be hung on knots tied in the appropriate place.

Colour plays an important part in attracting the interest of a child and the frame itself can be dyed and varnished, as can other wooden components. A non-toxic paint would be best for painting the tin and other objects.

CUTTING LIST

description	material	length	width	thickness	no. off	comments
Leg section (1)	Softwood	525mm (20½in)	60mm (2¼in)	12mm (½in)	4	Leg sections are shaped before being glued together
Leg section (2)	Softwood	465mm (18¼in)	30mm (1¼in)	12mm (½in)	4	,,
Top rail	Dowel	500mm (19¾in)	25mm (1in) diameter		1	The rail is cut in the middle to fit the spinning disc
Hand grip bars	Dowel	110mm (4¼in)	12mm (½in) diameter		2	
Spinning disc	Plywood	65mm (2½in) diameter		18mm (¾in)	1	The disc may be made by glueing thinner plywood discs together
Arms	Dowel	150mm (6in)	8mm (⅜in) diameter			
Wooden balls	Hardwood	25mm (1in) diameter			5	
Axle for disc	Dowel	120mm (4¾in)	12mm (½in) diameter		1	

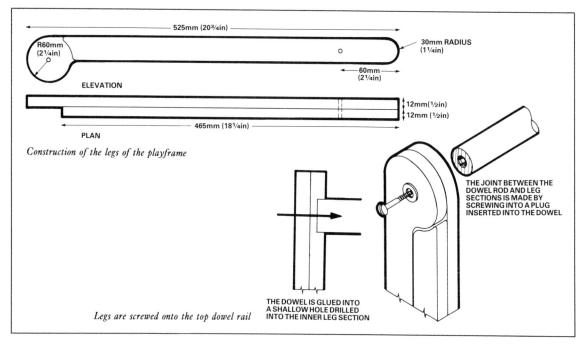

525mm (20¾in)

R60mm (2¼in)

30mm RADIUS (1¼in)

60mm (2¼in)

ELEVATION

12mm(½in)
12mm (½in)

465mm (18¼in)

PLAN

Construction of the legs of the playframe

THE JOINT BETWEEN THE DOWEL ROD AND LEG SECTIONS IS MADE BY SCREWING INTO A PLUG INSERTED INTO THE DOWEL

THE DOWEL IS GLUED INTO A SHALLOW HOLE DRILLED INTO THE INNER LEG SECTION

Legs are screwed onto the top dowel rail

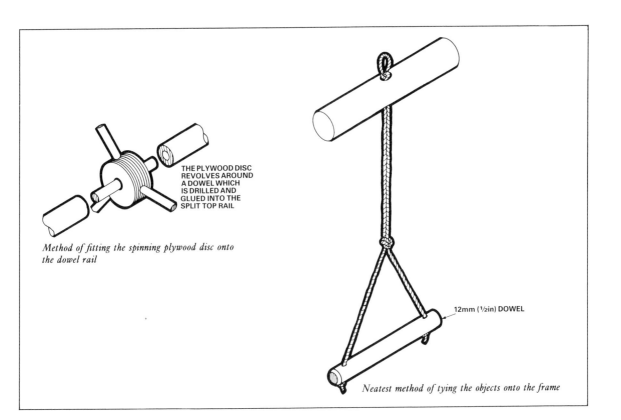

THE PLYWOOD DISC REVOLVES AROUND A DOWEL WHICH IS DRILLED AND GLUED INTO THE SPLIT TOP RAIL

Method of fitting the spinning plywood disc onto the dowel rail

12mm (½in) DOWEL

Neatest method of tying the objects onto the frame

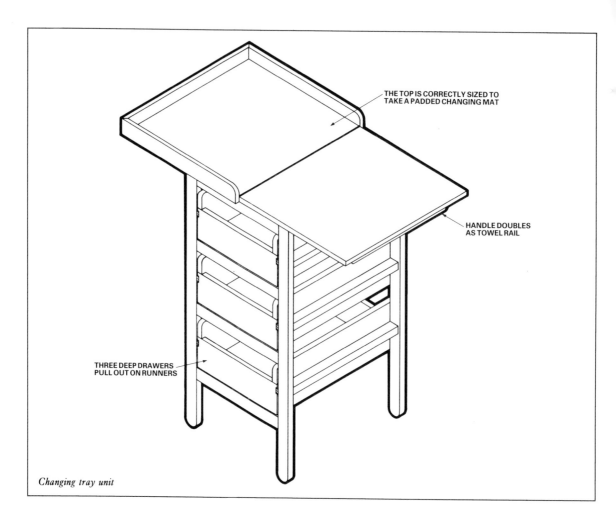

THE TOP IS CORRECTLY SIZED TO
TAKE A PADDED CHANGING MAT

HANDLE DOUBLES
AS TOWEL RAIL

THREE DEEP DRAWERS
PULL OUT ON RUNNERS

Changing tray unit

CHANGING TRAY UNIT
(Overall dimensions: 495 × 445 × 910mm high; $19\frac{1}{2}$ × $17\frac{1}{2}$ × $35\frac{3}{4}$in)

This changing tray unit is an extremely useful piece of nursery furniture and can be used for at least the first year of a baby's life. The folding and sliding top is correctly sized to take a padded changing mat and the lifting handle doubles as a towel rail when the top is opened. Beneath the changing tray are three deep drawers which can be pulled out on runners from either side of the unit. The drawers are deep enough to take the wide range of equipment associated with changing and dressing babies such as powder, cleansing lotion, cream, cotton wool, nappies, clothes, etc. Details of the changing unit are given in the orthographic drawing.

The unit is a hardwood construction and the underframe consists of four legs joined by front, back and side rails. The front and back rails may be jointed to the legs by dowel or mortise and tenon joints. The side rails, which double as drawer runners, should be dowel jointed in an offset position so that they project by 10mm ($\frac{3}{8}$in) into the internal space of the frame. It

should be noted that the lengths stated for these rails in the cutting list are shoulder to shoulder measurements and extra material should be added on to this length if mortise and tenon joints are to be used. The two top rails should be grooved along their inside faces before they are assembled in the frame and this groove should be 12mm ($\frac{1}{2}$in) wide, 8mm ($\frac{5}{16}$in) deep and started at a distance of 14mm ($\frac{9}{16}$in) from the top edge of the rails.

The three drawers consist of lap jointed boxes with shortened fronts which allow the drawer to be pulled out with the fingers and which also give a view to the contents of the drawers. The drawer sides are grooved to a depth of 8mm ($\frac{5}{16}$in) to slide along the runners built into the underframe and it is recommended that the bases of the drawers should be grooved into the drawer sides to give maximum strength to the drawers. The drawer bases are of hardboard and the smooth side of the hardboard should be painted white before being fitted, or white-faced hardboard used if it is available.

The folding and sliding top of the unit is made up of two melamine-faced chipboard panels hinged together. The board which is fitted to the top of the frame is

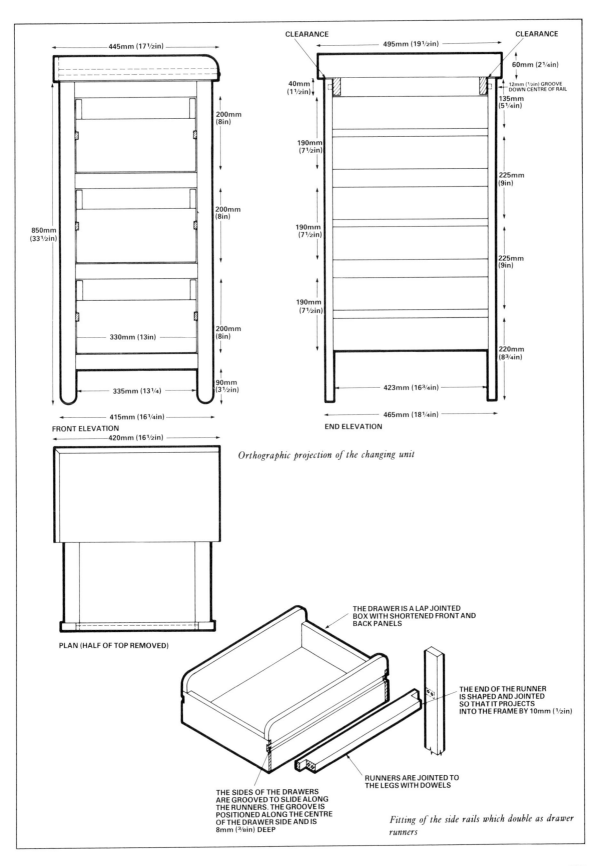

445mm (17½in)

850mm (33½in)

200mm (8in)

200mm (8in)

200mm (8in)

330mm (13in)

335mm (13¼)

90mm (3½in)

415mm (16¼in)

FRONT ELEVATION

CLEARANCE

CLEARANCE

495mm (19½in)

60mm (2¼in)

40mm (1½in)

12mm (½in) GROOVE DOWN CENTRE OF RAIL

135mm (5¼in)

190mm (7½in)

225mm (9in)

190mm (7½in)

225mm (9in)

190mm (7½in)

220mm (8¾in)

423mm (16¾in)

465mm (18¼in)

END ELEVATION

Orthographic projection of the changing unit

420mm (16½in)

PLAN (HALF OF TOP REMOVED)

THE DRAWER IS A LAP JOINTED BOX WITH SHORTENED FRONT AND BACK PANELS

THE END OF THE RUNNER IS SHAPED AND JOINTED SO THAT IT PROJECTS INTO THE FRAME BY 10mm (½in)

RUNNERS ARE JOINTED TO THE LEGS WITH DOWELS

THE SIDES OF THE DRAWERS ARE GROOVED TO SLIDE ALONG THE RUNNERS. THE GROOVE IS POSITIONED ALONG THE CENTRE OF THE DRAWER SIDE AND IS 8mm (³⁄₈in) DEEP

Fitting of the side rails which double as drawer runners

slightly larger than the folding flap and is edged with strips of hardwood which are mitred at the corners. The folding flap is hinged on a length of piano hinge or a pair of radiused hinges. If a piano hinge is to be used there is good sense in applying a hardwood edging strip onto the top panels where the hinge is to be screwed, to give the necessarily small gauge screws a stronger grip, in which case the sizes of the panels should be reduced accordingly.

To provide the sliding motion on the top, two battens are screwed edge-on underneath the top with counterbored screws. The hardwood sliding blocks are in turn screwed to these battens and must be positioned carefully to slide freely along the grooves, holding the top clear of the underframe by a couple of millimetres. Details of the dimensions and positions involved are given. Candle wax rubbed onto the sliding blocks and the grooves will supply a smooth gliding motion and may also be used on the drawers and runners.

A final refinement is to place self-adhesive pads onto the bottom surface of the folding flap so that when the flap is opened they cushion it as it rests on the tops of the legs and also hold it completely level with the sliding top.

Relevant techniques and chapter nos.

Dowel joints (3)
Lap joints (4)
Mortise and tenon joints (5)
Cutting grooves (10)
Counterbored screws (13)
Hinges (18)

CUTTING LIST

description	material	length	width	thickness	no. off	comments
Legs	Hardwood	850mm ($33\frac{1}{2}$in)	40mm ($1\frac{1}{2}$in)	21mm ($\frac{7}{8}$in)	4	The legs are rounded at the bottom
Rails	,,	335mm ($13\frac{1}{4}$in)	40mm ($1\frac{1}{2}$in)	15mm ($\frac{5}{8}$in)	8	Shoulder to shoulder lengths
Drawer runners	,,	465mm ($18\frac{1}{4}$in)	45mm ($1\frac{3}{4}$in)	15mm ($\frac{5}{8}$in)	6	
Top	Melamine-faced chipboard	470mm ($18\frac{1}{2}$in)	420mm ($16\frac{1}{2}$in)	16mm ($\frac{5}{8}$in)	1	Outward-facing edge is covered with edging strip
Folding top flap	,,	467mm ($18\frac{1}{4}$in)	418mm ($16\frac{1}{2}$in)	16mm ($\frac{5}{8}$in)	1	Edged all round with edging strip
Top surround	Hardwood					Jointed with mitres at the corners and screwed to the top
Sides	,,	445mm ($17\frac{1}{2}$in)	60mm ($2\frac{1}{4}$in)	12mm ($\frac{1}{2}$in)	2	
Back	,,	495mm ($19\frac{1}{2}$in)	60mm ($2\frac{1}{4}$in)	12mm ($\frac{1}{2}$in)	1	
Sliding mechanism	Hardwood					Screwed underneath the top with counterbored screws.
Battens	,,	420mm ($16\frac{1}{2}$in)	40mm ($1\frac{1}{2}$in)	21mm ($\frac{7}{8}$in)	2	
Blocks	,,	125mm (5in)	12mm ($\frac{1}{2}$in)	12mm ($\frac{1}{2}$in)	2	
Drawer sides	Hardwood	465mm ($18\frac{1}{4}$in)	190mm ($7\frac{1}{2}$in)	15mm ($\frac{5}{8}$in)	6	The drawers are constructed with lap joints
Drawer fronts and backs	,,	330mm (13in)	140mm ($5\frac{1}{2}$in)	15mm ($\frac{5}{8}$in)	6	,,
Drawer bases	Hardboard	450mm ($17\frac{3}{4}$in)	315mm ($12\frac{1}{2}$in)	3.5mm ($\frac{1}{8}$in)	3	The drawer bases are fitted into grooves in the drawers

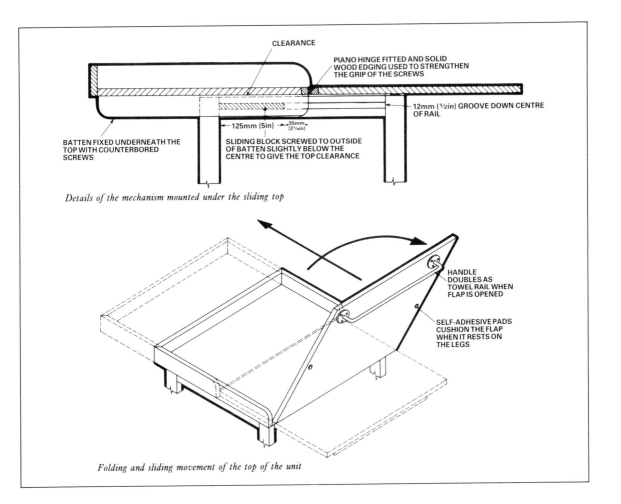

CLEARANCE

PIANO HINGE FITTED AND SOLID
WOOD EDGING USED TO STRENGTHEN
THE GRIP OF THE SCREWS

12mm (½in) GROOVE DOWN CENTRE
OF RAIL

125mm (5in) 55mm (2¼in)

BATTEN FIXED UNDERNEATH THE
TOP WITH COUNTERBORED
SCREWS

SLIDING BLOCK SCREWED TO OUTSIDE
OF BATTEN SLIGHTLY BELOW THE
CENTRE TO GIVE THE TOP CLEARANCE

Details of the mechanism mounted under the sliding top

HANDLE
DOUBLES AS
TOWEL RAIL WHEN
FLAP IS OPENED

SELF-ADHESIVE PADS
CUSHION THE FLAP
WHEN IT RESTS ON
THE LEGS

Folding and sliding movement of the top of the unit

26 Surfaces

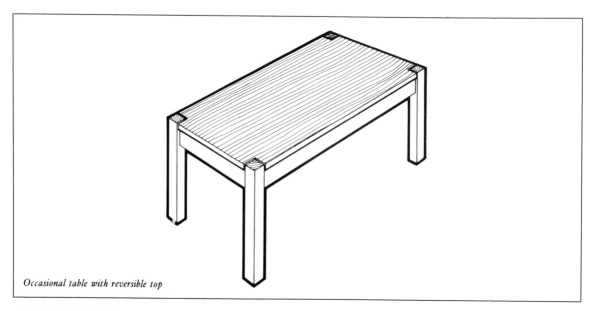

Occasional table with reversible top

OCCASIONAL TABLE WITH REVERSIBLE TOP
(Overall dimensions: 900 × 468 × 410mm high; 35½ × 18½ × 16¼in)

This occasional table consists of a simple leg and rail construction but the design has the advantage of a reversible top. One face of the top is a varnished or polished wood veneer and the other side is covered with plastic laminate, so that the most suitable surface may be turned uppermost to meet the needs of the moment. The materials for the frame may be of softwood or hardwood and the veneered chipboard for the top

CUTTING LIST

description	material	length	width	thickness	no. off	comments
Legs	Softwood or hardwood	410mm (16¼in)	45mm (1¾in)	45mm (1¾in)	4	May be tapered below rail joint
Top side rails	,,	810mm (32in)	75mm (3in)	20mm (⅞in)	2	The length is a shoulder to shoulder measurement
Top end rails	,,	378mm (15in)	75mm (3in)	20mm (⅞in)	2	,,
Top	Veneered chipboard	890mm (35in)	458mm (18in)	16mm (⅝in)	1	The top is shaped before being lipped all round
Covering	Plastic laminate	900mm (35½in)	468mm (18½in)	2mm (⅛in)	1	The laminate sheet is fixed with adhesive and then trimmed flush
Lipping	Softwood or hardwood	Aprox. 3000mm (118in)	16mm (⅝in)	5mm (¼in)		The lipping is fitted over-size for width and planed flush

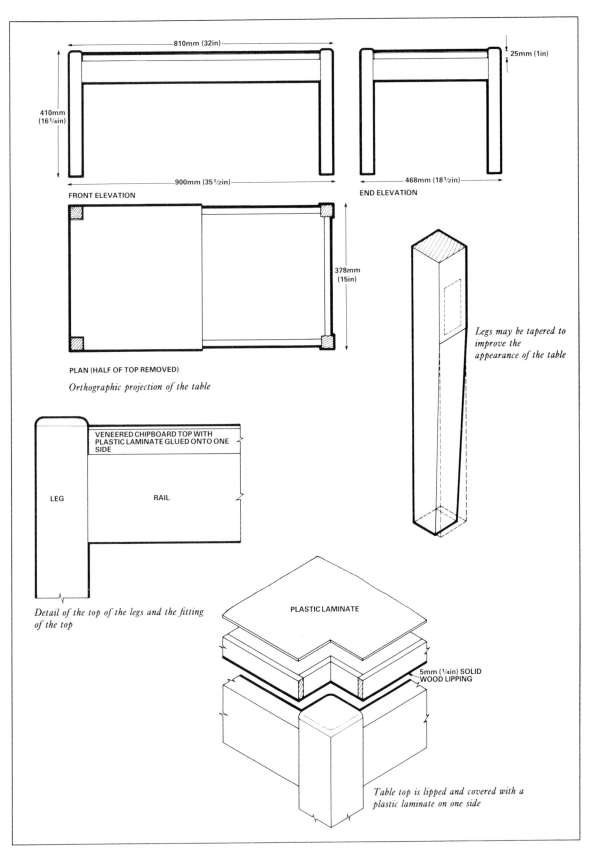

810mm (32in)

25mm (1in)

410mm (16¼in)

900mm (35½in)

FRONT ELEVATION

468mm (18½in)

END ELEVATION

378mm (15in)

PLAN (HALF OF TOP REMOVED)

Orthographic projection of the table

Legs may be tapered to improve the appearance of the table

VENEERED CHIPBOARD TOP WITH PLASTIC LAMINATE GLUED ONTO ONE SIDE

LEG

RAIL

Detail of the top of the legs and the fitting of the top

PLASTIC LAMINATE

5mm (¼in) SOLID WOOD LIPPING

Table top is lipped and covered with a plastic laminate on one side

bought to match. A general arrangement drawing of the table is given.

The frame of the table can be constructed with dowel or shouldered mortise and tenon joints, the rails being positioned centrally across the thickness of the legs. The lengths of the rails given in the cutting list are shoulder to shoulder measurements and extra material should be added if mortise and tenon joints are to be used. The top edges of the legs are generously rounded to give a neat appearance and to provide a lead-in for the top as it is lowered into place. If you like, the legs can be tapered below the rail joint on the inside faces to lessen their visual weight. The veneered chipboard top is edged with 5mm ($\frac{1}{4}$in) lipping strip to match the veneer on the board, then the less attractive side is covered with a plastic laminate of a chosen colour or pattern.

Relevant techniques and chapter nos.

Dowel joints (3)
Mortise and tenon joints (5)
Lipping manufactured board (11)

GARDEN TABLE
(Overall dimensions: 700mm diameter × 690mm high; 27½ × 25in)

The construction method of this table is such that it can easily be dismantled into three sections and can therefore be stored in the house or garage and saved the rigours of continuous exposure to the elements. The table is intended as a softwood construction, although it may equally be made in hardwood, and it will be important to apply a suitable finish to ensure a long life in outside conditions.

The overall dimensions and construction of the table are shown in the orthographic drawing. The pedestal consists of a pair of cross-halved top rails and a pair of cross-halved bottom rails spaced apart by four 34 × 34mm ($1\frac{3}{8}$ × $1\frac{3}{8}$in) lengths of timber. These components are assembled into two sections which will slide into one another and lock into a firm pedestal support for the table top. Dowel joints are the most suitable jointing method for constructing these sections and it must be remembered that an adhesive which is able to withstand outside conditions should be used.

The rails should be shaped to make their appearance as attractive as possible and some design examples are given. In shaping the bottom rails an attempt should be made to form feet rather than leaving a straight edge along the bottom, as this will greatly increase the stability of the table when it is standing on uneven ground. The four uprights in the pedestal section may also be made more attractive by rounding or chamfering the outward-facing corner of each.

The supporting frame for the table top consists of six lengths of softwood jointed with halving joints into a square frame with two crossing members. Before the table top boards are screwed onto this frame the pedestal location strips should be screwed into place through the frame. It would also be advisable to drill the holes which will take the locating dowels before fitting the strips. When the table top boards are screwed into place onto the supporting frame a number of strips of wood 15mm ($\frac{5}{8}$in) in width would be useful to place between the boards to establish the 15mm ($\frac{5}{8}$in) spaces accurately. It is recommended that the boards should be cut slightly over the lengths stated in the cutting list and screwed into position on the supporting frame. Once in place the

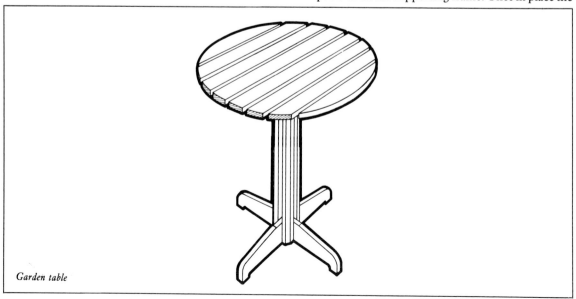

Garden table

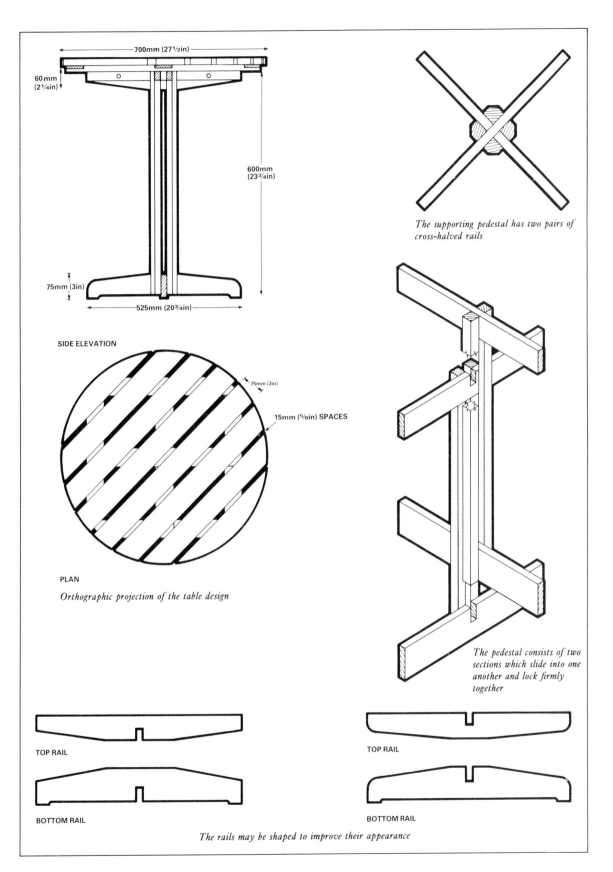

700mm (27½in)

60 mm
(2¼in)

600mm
(23¾in)

75mm (3in)

525mm (20¾in)

SIDE ELEVATION

The supporting pedestal has two pairs of cross-halved rails

75mm (3in)

15mm (⅝in) SPACES

PLAN

Orthographic projection of the table design

The pedestal consists of two sections which slide into one another and lock firmly together

TOP RAIL

BOTTOM RAIL

TOP RAIL

BOTTOM RAIL

The rails may be shaped to improve their appearance

123

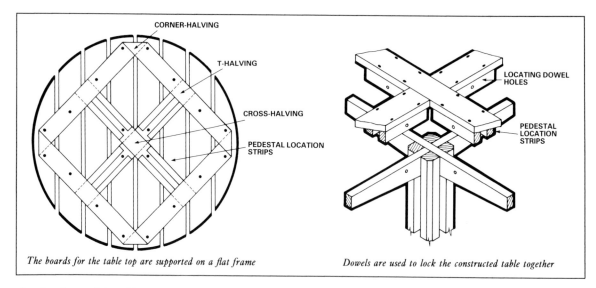

CORNER-HALVING

T-HALVING

CROSS-HALVING

PEDESTAL LOCATION
STRIPS

LOCATING DOWEL
HOLES

PEDESTAL
LOCATION
STRIPS

The boards for the table top are supported on a flat frame

Dowels are used to lock the constructed table together

circular shape of the table top can be drawn with a pencil on a piece of string, pinned at the centre of the table top. Each board may then be removed, shaped correctly and replaced until the whole top is to shape.

When the holes have been drilled into the top cross rails to take the 6mm ($\frac{1}{4}$in) locating dowels the completed table may be constructed and locked into position.

Relevant techniques and chapter nos.

Dowel joints (3)
Halving joints (4)
Preparation for screws (13)
Finishes (14)

CUTTING LIST

description	material	length	width	thickness	no. off	comments
Legs	Softwood	650mm (25$\frac{1}{2}$in)	34mm (1$\frac{1}{4}$in)	34mm (1$\frac{1}{4}$in)	4	The outward-facing corner of the legs may be rounded or chamfered
Bottom cross rails	,,	525mm (20$\frac{1}{2}$in)	75mm (3in)	21mm ($\frac{7}{8}$in)	2	These rails are jointed with a cross-halving and shaped as required
Top cross rails	,,	525mm (20$\frac{1}{2}$in)	60mm (2$\frac{1}{4}$in)	21mm ($\frac{7}{8}$in)	2	,,
Table top	,,	700mm (27$\frac{1}{2}$in)	75mm (3in)	15mm ($\frac{5}{8}$in)	2	The table top boards
,,	,,	675mm (26$\frac{1}{2}$in)	75mm (3in)	15mm ($\frac{5}{8}$in)	2	are set 15mm ($\frac{5}{8}$in)
,,	,,	600mm (23$\frac{1}{2}$in)	75mm (3in)	15mm ($\frac{5}{8}$in)	2	apart, and are fitted
,,	,,	425mm (16$\frac{3}{4}$in)	75mm (3in)	15mm ($\frac{5}{8}$in)	2	by screwing up through the support frame
Support frame members	,,	535mm (21in)	60mm (2$\frac{1}{4}$in)	15mm ($\frac{5}{8}$in)	6	Corner- and T-halvings are used to joint the support frame
Pedestal location strips	,,	160mm (6$\frac{1}{4}$in)	30mm (1$\frac{1}{4}$in)	21mm ($\frac{7}{8}$in)	8	These are screwed to the support frame
Locating dowels	Dowel rod	75mm (3in)	6mm ($\frac{1}{4}$in) diameter		4	

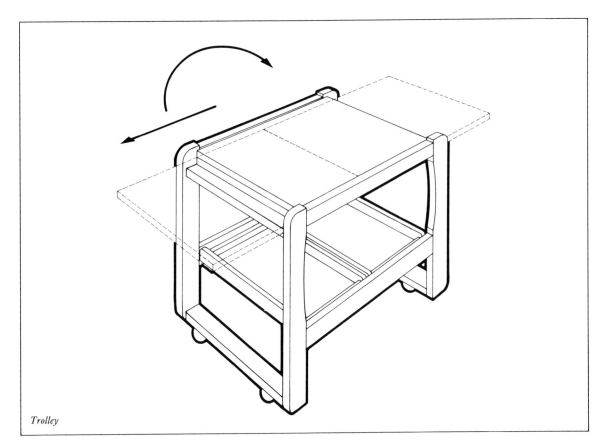

Trolley

TROLLEY
(Overall dimensions: 640 × 452 × 650mm high; 25¼ × 17¾ × 25½in)

A major factor in the design of this trolley has been the desire to provide the largest possible area on which to set out a tea, a buffet or drinks, on a piece of furniture which should not take up too much space when not in use. This has been achieved with a sliding and folding top which doubles its surface area when it is opened out and yet does not look out of place when it is folded away.

The constructional details of the trolley are shown on the orthographic drawings. The upper and lower side rails are jointed to the vertical corner members with mortise and tenon or dowel joints, the upper rails being grooved to accept the dowels which are set into the edges of the lower surface board and which control the sliding movement. (It should be noted that the lengths for both the side and cross rails in the cutting list are shoulder to shoulder measurements and extra material should be added if certain jointing methods are chosen, e.g. mortise and tenon joints.) The joints between the cross rails and the vertical corner members may also be dowel joints, but perhaps consideration should be given to the possibility of using one of the flush K.D. fittings. The reason for this is that the fittings would allow the trolley frame to be easily constructed around the sliding and folding top, rather than being glued and therefore

assembled permanently with the top in place. This may be important if the frame has to be dismantled to allow adjustments or maintenance to be carried out on the top mechanism.

The sizes given in the cutting list for the two top surfaces are finished sizes and should be adjusted accordingly if solid wood lipping is to be applied to finish the edges. The use of solid wood is recommended as it would allow a small finger hole to be fashioned to aid the unfolding of the upper surface and would also provide a stronger fixing for the dowels which are set into the edge of the lower surface. The dowels should be fitted into the positions indicated and the two surface boards hinged together with a pair of radiused hinges.

The two trays which rest on supporting strips inside the lower side rails are easily removable for serving drinks or for eating a lap meal. Each tray consists of a lap-jointed frame which is rebated around the bottom edge, and into this rebate a plywood panel is fitted. The supporting strips are screwed into place along the bottom edge of the lower side rails.

The trolley is made mobile by fitting four castors of a suitable load-carrying capacity with plate fittings onto the lower cross rails. The appearance of the trolley can be refined by rounding the outward-facing corners of the vertical corner members at the top and bottom and by shaping the corner members between the jointing

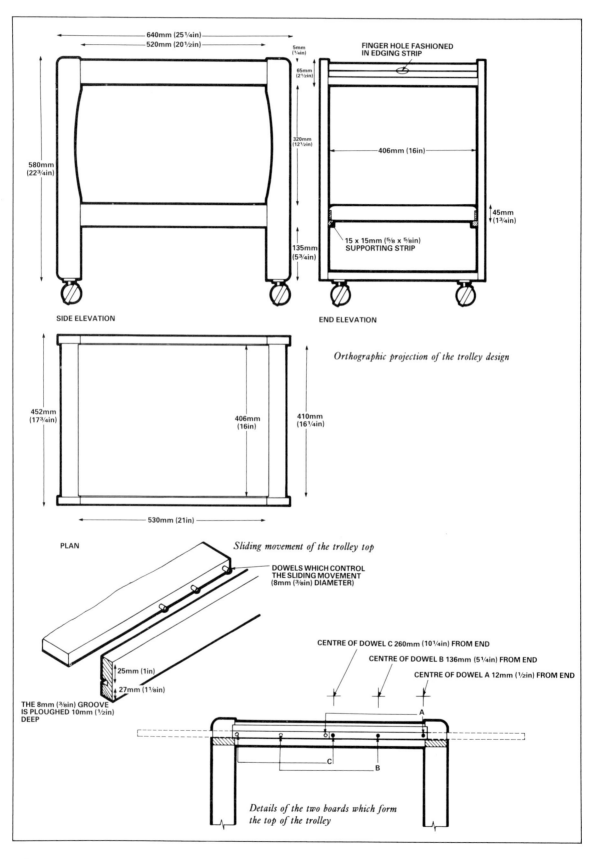

640mm (25¼in)

520mm (20½in)

5mm (¼in)

65mm (2½in)

FINGER HOLE FASHIONED IN EDGING STRIP

320mm (12½in)

406mm (16in)

580mm (22¾in)

45mm (1¾in)

135mm (5¾in)

15 x 15mm (⅝ x ⅝in) SUPPORTING STRIP

SIDE ELEVATION

END ELEVATION

Orthographic projection of the trolley design

452mm (17¾in)

406mm (16in)

410mm (16¼in)

530mm (21in)

PLAN

Sliding movement of the trolley top

DOWELS WHICH CONTROL THE SLIDING MOVEMENT (8mm (⅜in) DIAMETER)

25mm (1in)

27mm (1⅛in)

THE 8mm (⅜in) GROOVE IS PLOUGHED 10mm (½in) DEEP

CENTRE OF DOWEL C 260mm (10¼in) FROM END

CENTRE OF DOWEL B 136mm (5¼in) FROM END

CENTRE OF DOWEL A 12mm (½in) FROM END

A

C

B

Details of the two boards which form the top of the trolley

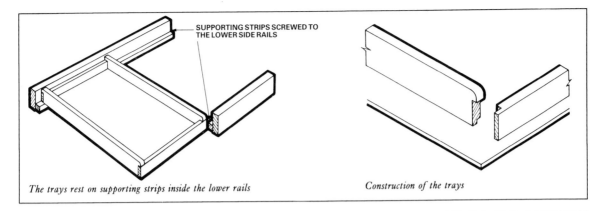

SUPPORTING STRIPS SCREWED TO THE LOWER SIDE RAILS

The trays rest on supporting strips inside the lower rails

Construction of the trays

positions of the upper and lower side rails. Both of these operations should be carried out before the trolley is finally assembled.

Relevant techniques and chapter nos.

Dowel joints (3)
Lap joints (4)
Mortise and tenon joints (5)
Cutting grooves and rebates (10)
Edging manufactured board (11)
K.D. fittings (12)
Castors and hinges (18)

CUTTING LIST

description	material	length	width	thickness	no. off	comments
Vertical corner members	Softwood or hardwood	580mm (22¾in)	6omm (2¼in)	21mm (⅞in)	4	The legs may be shaped between the upper and lower side rail joints
Upper and lower side rails	,,	520mm (20½in)	6omm (2¼in)	21mm (⅞in)	4	The length given is a shoulder to shoulder measurement. The upper rails are grooved to accept the dowels which are set into the sliding top
Upper and lower cross rails	,,	410mm (16¼in)	50mm (2in)	21mm (⅞in)	4	The length given is a shoulder to shoulder measurement
Top surfaces	Veneered or melamine-faced chipboard	530mm (21in)	405mm (16in)	16mm (⅝in)	2	These measurements include edging all round
Tray support strips	Softwood or hardwood	520mm (20½in)	15mm (⅝in)	15mm (⅝in)	2	These are screwed along the bottom edge of the inside face of the lower side rails
Tray sides	Softwood or hardwood	406mm (16in)	45mm (1¾in)	12mm (½in)	4	The tray sides and ends are jointed with lap joints, and are rebated along the bottom edge
Tray ends	,,	260mm (10¼in)	30mm (1¼in)	12mm (½in)	4	
Tray bases	Plywood	394mm (15½in)	248mm (9¾in)	6mm (¼in)	2	The tray bases are pinned and glued into the rebate in the bottom of the tray frames

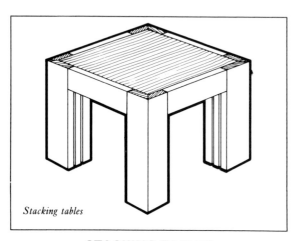

Stacking tables

STACKING TABLES
(Overall dimensions: 450 × 450 × 420mm high; 17¾ × 17¾ × 16½in)

The appearance of these stacking tables when they are not individually in use has been an important consideration in their design. It is for this reason that the tables cover each other when stacked and the overall appearance is of one unit. The construction method used to make the large and medium tables is the same but the small table is made in a different way as the cross-sections of the legs and rails are quite different.

When making the large and medium tables the four side frames are jointed and assembled as flat frames. The joints used in constructing these frames will most probably be dowel joints and it would be wise to leave a little surplus material on the top of the leg to allow the frame to be planed flush after assembly. A groove is

ploughed along the top of each frame to accept the top support panel at a distance of 12mm (½in) from the top edge, and the 45° mitres are planed along the outside edges of the legs to form the corner joints. The table top of veneered plywood is glued onto the 6mm (¼in) plywood support panel, and when the table is finally assembled will lie completely flush with the tops of the four side frames.

Once all the work on the frames and top has been completed the whole table is glued and assembled in one operation. The table can be held together with sash cramps, but it would be easier to use web clamps or loops of cord or string, with wooden blocks pushed towards the corners for tension.

The joints between the rails and legs on the small table will again most probably be dowel joints, but the table top in this case rests on supporting strips which are pinned and glued onto the inside faces of the rails, in the appropriate position. To complete the rebate which holds the veneered plywood top a corner of the leg must be carefully chiselled out, and this is probably best done when the table frame has been assembled and the supporting strips have been fitted so that the depth and width which have to be removed can be accurately established.

Relevant techniques and chapter nos.

Dowel joints (3)
Cutting grooves (10)
Glueing and cramping up (15)

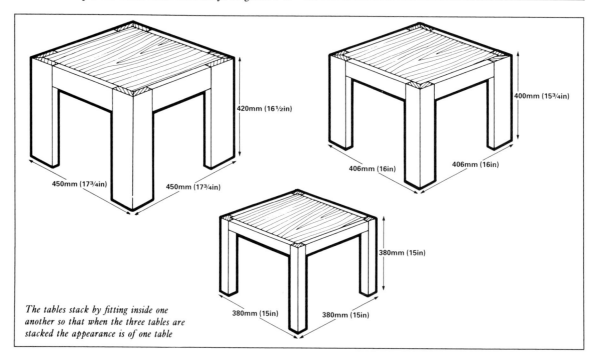

420mm (16½in)

450mm (17¾in)   450mm (17¾in)

400mm (15¾in)

406mm (16in)   406mm (16in)

380mm (15in)

380mm (15in)   380mm (15in)

The tables stack by fitting inside one another so that when the three tables are stacked the appearance is of one table

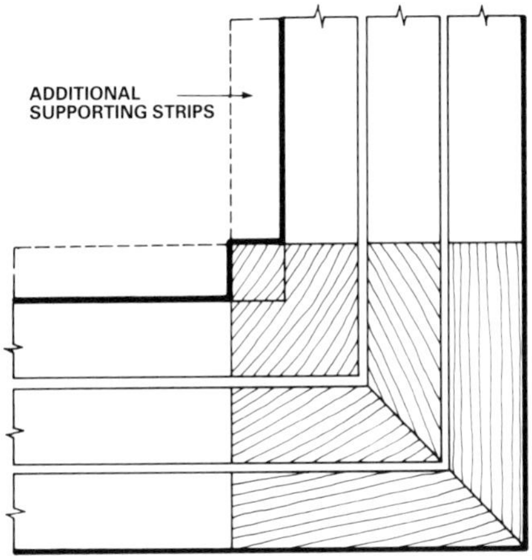
ADDITIONAL
SUPPORTING STRIPS

Basic construction of each of the tables

For the medium and large tables the side frames are firstly assembled as flat frames

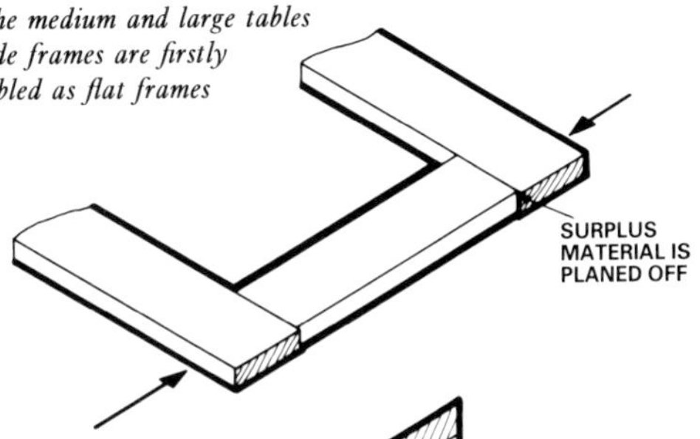
SURPLUS
MATERIAL IS
PLANED OFF

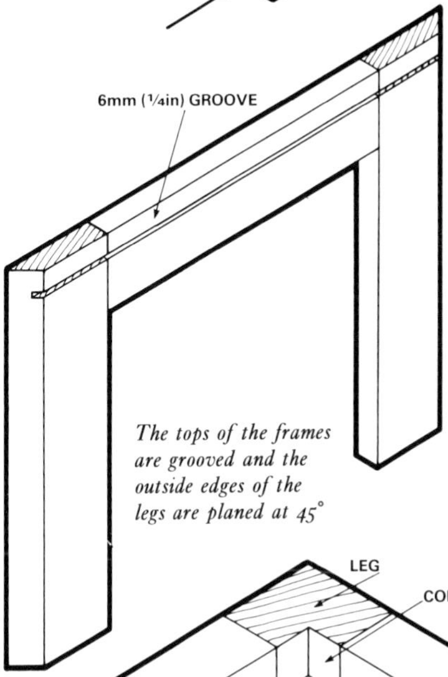
6mm (¼in) GROOVE

The tops of the frames are grooved and the outside edges of the legs are planed at 45°

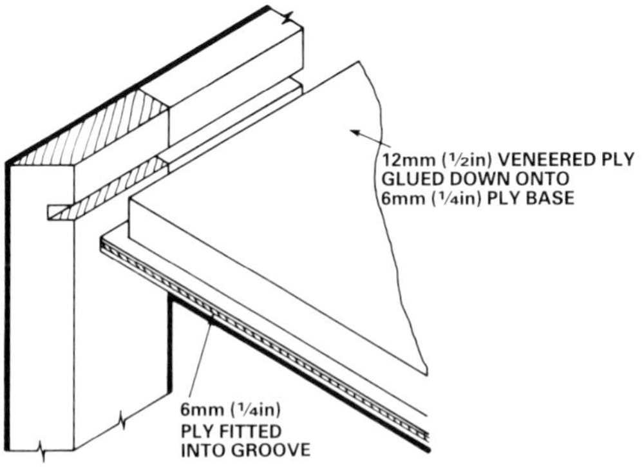
12mm (½in) VENEERED PLY
GLUED DOWN ONTO
6mm (¼in) PLY BASE
6mm (¼in)
PLY FITTED
INTO GROOVE

Detail of the fitting of the table top

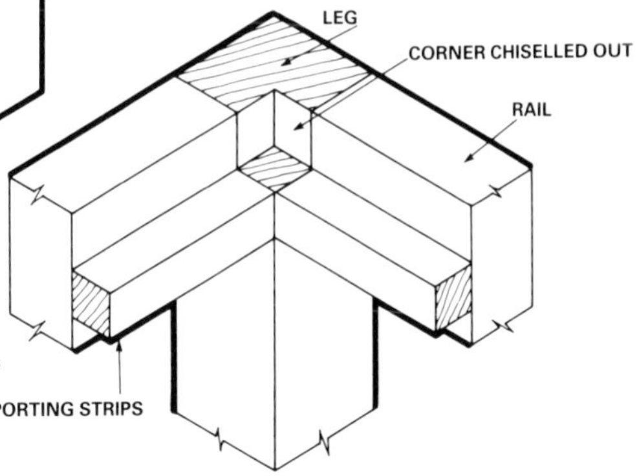
LEG
CORNER CHISELLED OUT
RAIL
SUPPORTING STRIPS

View inside the corner of the small table

CUTTING LIST

description	material	length	width	thickness	no. off	comments
Large table						
Legs	Softwood or hardwood	420mm (16½in)	80mm (3¼in)	20mm (⅞in)	8	
Top rails	”	290mm (11½in)	80mm (3¼in)	20mm (⅞in)	4	290mm (11½in) is a shoulder to shoulder measurement
Top	Veneered plywood	410mm (16¼in)	410mm (16¼in)	12mm (½in)	1	The top is glued to its supporting panel
Top support panel	Plywood	422mm (16½in)	422mm (16½in)	6mm (¼in)	1	This panel is fitted into the groove cut around the inside of the frame

(*cont.*)

description	material	length	width	thickness	no. off	comments
Medium table						
Legs	Softwood or hardwood	400mm (15$\frac{3}{4}$in)	58mm (2$\frac{1}{4}$in)	20mm ($\frac{7}{8}$in)	8	
Top rails	,,	290mm (11$\frac{1}{2}$in)	60mm (2$\frac{1}{4}$in)	20mm ($\frac{7}{8}$in)	4	290mm (11$\frac{1}{2}$in) is a shoulder to shoulder measurement
Top	Veneered plywood	366mm (14$\frac{1}{2}$in)	366mm (14$\frac{1}{2}$in)	12mm ($\frac{1}{2}$in)	1	The top is glued to its supporting panel
Top support panel	Plywood	378mm (15in)	375mm (15in)	6mm ($\frac{1}{4}$in)	1	This panel is fitted into the groove cut around the inside of the frame
Small table						
Legs	Softwood or hardwood	380mm (15in)	35mm (1$\frac{1}{4}$in)	35mm (1$\frac{1}{4}$in)	8	
Top rails	,,	290mm (11$\frac{1}{2}$in)	40mm (1$\frac{1}{2}$in)	20mm ($\frac{7}{8}$in)	4	290mm (11$\frac{1}{2}$in) is a shoulder to shoulder measurement
Top	Veneered plywood	320mm (12$\frac{1}{2}$in)	320mm (12$\frac{1}{2}$in)	12mm ($\frac{1}{2}$in)	1	
Top support strips	Softwood or hardwood	290mm (11$\frac{1}{2}$in)	15mm ($\frac{5}{8}$in)	15mm ($\frac{5}{8}$in)	4	Strips are pinned and glued to the inside of the frame

Glossary

A

abrasive hard, graded material stuck onto paper or cloth backing and used to rub down and smooth surfaces.

air seasoning method of drying timber by stacking boards in the open, under a simple roof.

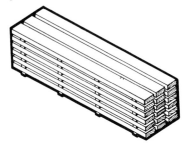

aluminium oxide abrasive material used mainly on the belts and discs of sanding machinery

annual ring growth ring evident on the cross-section of a tree formed by the contrast between the light coloured spring growth and the darker summer/autumn growth.

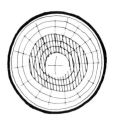

auger a term used to describe a tool with a twisted shank which can bore holes in wood.

awl a hand tool with a sharp, pointed blade which is used to mark out hole centres and cutting lines.

B

back saw term used to describe a saw which has a thin blade supported by a fold of metal along the top, e.g. tenon saw.

banding narrow strips of wood often used for inlay work.

bandsaw motor driven sawing machine which has a continuous blade running on two or three pulleys. The machine is particularly useful for cutting curves.

batten a general term used to describe softwood sections.

battenboard a manufactured board material consisting of wide softwood core strips held between veneers.

bead narrow half-round moulding feature.

beeswax a wax which makes an excellent polish for wood. It can be dissolved in turpentine to ease application.

belt sander a sanding machine with a continuous belt which is particularly useful for sanding large areas.

bench hook a sawing board which can be hooked over the edge of the bench or held in the vice.

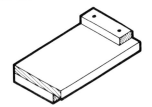

bench stop a square wooden peg which can be raised through the bench top and against which timber is planed or sanded.

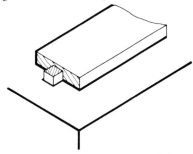

bits tools used to bore holes whilst being held in a carpenter's brace.

block plane a small metal plane which is particularly useful for fine work and for working across the grain.

blockboard a manufactured board material, with softwood core strips no wider than 25mm (1in) sandwiched between veneers.

board a sawn piece of timber under 50mm (2in) thick.

bow saw a saw of ancient origins used to cut curves in thicker material.

brace (carpenter's) a cranked tool used to drive boring bits.

bradawl a hand tool with a sharpened square end used to bore small holes in preparation for the insertion of screws or large nails.

bridle joints a group of joints in which the thickness of the joint members is divided into three. (Ch.6)

bull-nose shoulder plane a small plane with a low-angled blade, suitable for planing the shoulders of joints and for work on stopped rebates.

burr the wire edge left on a chisel or plane blade after sharpening which must be removed by backing off.

butt hinge common form of door hinge. (Ch.18)

butt joint edge joint simply made by glueing square-edged boards together. (Ch.9)

button hardwood block used to fix a solid wood table top to its underframe. Fitted correctly, buttons will allow for the expansion and contraction of the top.

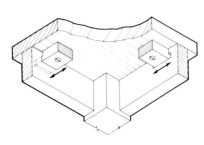

C

cabinet scraper a tool used to finish a surface which scrapes away fine shavings. It is particularly helpful when working irregular or awkward grain.

calipers two-legged instrument used to measure internal and external dimensions, in particular the diameters of cylinders or holes.

cap iron the steel plate which supports the blade in a bench plane.

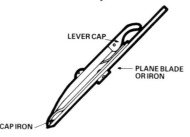

castor a small wheel or roller which is fitted to make items of furniture moveable. (Ch.18)

centre bit a bit used to cut shallow holes of quite large diameters.

chamfer the removal of a corner or edge for decoration or to protect the edge from damage.

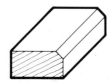

checks cracks or tears in the structure of wood often caused by too rapid kiln seasoning.

cheek the waste material on the sides of a tenon or the gripping surface in a vice jaw.

chipboard (particle board) a manufactured board material made by bonding chips of wood together under heat and pressure. (Ch.1)

chisels a range of tools which are used to cut, shape and trim timber. The three most common types of chisel are the firmer, the bevel-edge and the mortise.

FIRMER CHISEL

BEVEL-EDGE CHISEL

MORTISE CHISEL

chuck the part of the drill or brace which grips the drilling tool or bit.

circular plane a plane which has a sole made of thin spring steel which can be adjusted to work on convex or concave curves of a large radius.

clamp a wooden member fixed across end grain to prevent warping.

claw hammer a hammer which has the facility of being able to extract nails.

clearance hole the hole drilled in a piece of wood to accept the shank of a screw. (Ch.13)

clenching to bend the protruding point of a nail back into the wood, across the grain.

coach screw large square-headed screws which are used in heavy exterior construction work. (Ch.13)

cock bead a moulding strip which is often applied to drawer edges.

comb joint a joint with a large glue-ing area which is often used in box construction.

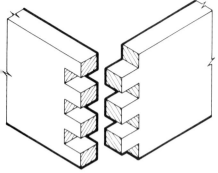

combination square a square which can be used to mark or test angles of 45° or 90°.

conditioning the adjustment of the moisture content in timber to match the humidity in the area where it is to be used.
conversion the process of sawing logs into useful timber. Different methods produce different qualities and sizes of board.

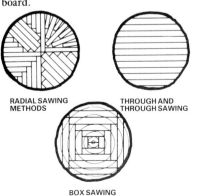

RADIAL SAWING METHODS   THROUGH AND THROUGH SAWING

BOX SAWING

coping saw a saw which has a fine blade held in tension which is used for cutting curves in thin material.

counter veneer (balancing veneer) a veneer which is applied on the opposite side to a face veneer to maintain stability.

counterbore a hole which is drilled to accept a screw.

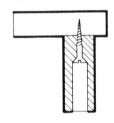

countersink the tool used to cut the hollow to accept a countersink head screw.

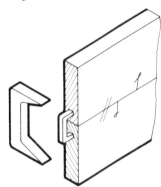

cradle a piece of workshop equipment which is used to hold square-section timber, when the corners are to be planed off. (Ch.2)
creosote a tar-based preservative for fencing and exterior joinery.
cross-cut saw a saw which has teeth which are shaped and sharpened to cut cleanly across the grain.

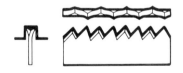

cupping the result of a board warping across its width.

cutting gauge a gauge which is fitted with a blade and which is used to mark shoulder lines across the grain. The gauge can also be used to cut small rebates along the grain.

D
dog a metal staple which can be used to hold edge joints under pressure when glueing.

dovetail a tapered shape cut in wood which is the basis of dovetail jointing.
dovetail saw a small backsaw which is used for fine work including the cutting of dovetail joints.
dovetail template a metal template which is useful for marking out the slopes of dovetails in joints.
dowel rod rod of birch or ramin which is available in a range of diameters. A useful constructional or jointing material.
dye a spirit or water-based colourant which is used to deepen the natural colour of timber or to imitate a different timber.

E
edge joint a joint between two boards used to achieve a greater width of material. (Ch.9)
expansive bit a bit which is capable of being adjusted to the required diameter. (Ch.16)
extension bar a bar which can be fitted to a sash cramp to extend it.

F

face edge the edge which is planed straight and square to the face side when planing timber to size. (Ch.2)

face side the first surface to be planed true when preparing timber. All measurements and markings are made from this side (Ch.2)

figure the decorative markings on wood which result from the grain.

flatbit a drilling bit which is used in a power drill and is often used for large diameter holes.

flushmount a neat and useful K.D. fitting. (Ch.12)

former a shaped block used for forming materials into shape, e.g. heated acrylic sheet or laminated veneers.

fox wedging a method of wedging a joint in which the wedges themselves are hidden inside the joint.

french polishing a traditional method of polishing furniture to a high gloss using shellac materials.

fretsaw a frame saw with a deep frame and a fine blade used to cut intricate shapes and designs; hence fretwork.

G

garnet paper a reddish coloured abrasive paper which although more expensive is long-lasting and efficient.

gauge number the gauge number of a screw indicates the thickness of the shank of the screw, e.g. a gauge 10 screw has a shank diameter of 5mm ($\frac{3}{16}$in).

glasspaper an abrasive paper consisting of crushed glass glued to a paper backing.

gouges tools with curved-section blades used to cut curves and for hollowing out. There are two types, the scribing gouge and the firmer gouge.

SCRIBING GOUGE

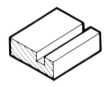

FIRMER GOUGE

green timber a term used to describe wet timber, i.e. timber which has not been seasoned.

grinding angle the angle which is ground on the end of a chisel or plane blade before sharpening. The grinding angle is normally between 20° and 25°.

groove a trench cut into a piece of wood to hold a panel, partition or base.

H

halving joints flush joints in which half of each joint member is removed. (Ch.4)

hammer a striking tool used to drive nails and to strike punches. The Warrington cross pein hammer is best for general purposes.

hand drill a geared drilling tool used with small diameter twist drills.

hand saw a term used to describe saws which consist of a long steel blade with a wooden or plastic handle fitted. The rip saw, cross-cut and panel saw fall into this category.

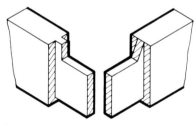

handscrew a cramp which has wooden jaws which spread the pressure over a large area and are capable of holding awkward shapes.

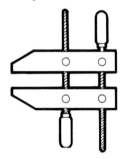

hardboard a manufactured board material made by compressing a wood pulp and glue mixture. (Ch.1)

hardener a liquid or paste used to promote the setting of a resin or adhesive.

hardwood a botanical term used to identify trees which are as a rule broad-leaved and deciduous. Timber from these trees is usually physically hard.

hasp and staple a fitting used in conjunction with a padlock to keep the doors of sheds and outbuildings securely closed.

haunch the piece of material left in above a tenon at a corner joint to give support to the full width of the rail. The haunch may be square or sloping. (Ch.5)

heartwood the inner part of the tree which does not contain living cells and is darker and more durable than the outer sapwood layer. The heartwood yields the timber which is used for furniture making.

holdfast a cramping device which is used to hold a workpiece down onto the bench top.

honing the sharpening of the blade of a cutting tool.

honing guide a tool which is used to maintain the correct sharpening angle when honing a plane or chisel blade.

horn the surplus material which is left above a mortise during the cutting and assembling of the joint, to prevent splitting out at the top of the joint. The horn is trimmed off after assembly.

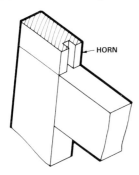

— HORN

housing joints a group of joints which allow shelves or panels to be housed into trenches cut into the side or base members. (Ch.7)

I

inlay decorative work which involves setting pieces of different types of wood into shaped recesses.

insulation board (softboard) a lightweight board material made from wood pulp and used on ceilings and walls. (Ch.1)

J

jack plane a medium-sized bench plane which is used for most general planing operations.

japanning a black, glossy protective lacquer found on screws and fittings which are to be used out of doors.

jig saw a portable power saw which is particularly useful for dividing up and shaping board materials.

K

kerf the groove in the wood made by a saw.

keying the setting of strips of wood into a joint to strengthen and support it.

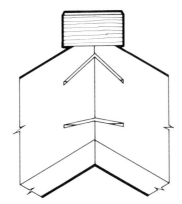

kicker a strip of wood fixed inside a cabinet above a drawer side to prevent the drawer falling as it is pulled out.

kiln seasoning the process by which timber is seasoned quickly in an oven, under carefully controlled conditions of temperature and humidity.

knots a feature in wood found where a branch was growing from the main trunk. A live knot may be considered a decorative feature but a dead knot will often be discoloured and may fall from the board, leaving a hole.

knotting a shellac and methylated spirit solution which is used to seal knots which may release resin and discolour the painted finish.

L

laminate a term used to describe the thin sheet materials which are found on worktops and table surfaces. These materials are often patterned and are heat and moisture proof.

lamination the process of building up a section or shape by glueing together thin layers or veneers.

laminboard a manufactured board material consisting of narrow softwood core strips sandwiched between veneers. A highly stable constructional material.

lap joint a joint in which one member overlaps or covers the other.

latex foam a rubber-based foam material used for mattresses and cushioning in furniture.

laying off the final brush strokes made in a varnish or paint to smooth the finish.

lever cap the sprung plate which holds the blade assembly in position in a plane (fig.471).

light a frame containing glass in a window or door.

lines narrow strips of material used in inlay work.

lipping strips of solid wood used to edge manufactured board materials.

M

mallet a tool used to strike chisels and gouges for cutting, and to aid job assembly.

marking knife a small knife used to mark out cutting lines on wood.

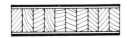

mirror plate a wall fixing plate which is screwed to the back of a frame. (Ch.18)

mitre the angle cut on the end of a joint member to make a mitred joint.

mitre block a wooden block with guiding saw cuts at 45° to help the accurate cutting of mitres.

mitre box an open-ended box which is used as a sawing guide for mitres on wide material.

mitre cramp a cramp used to hold a mitred joint together while the glue sets or while pins are driven in. (The model shown also incorporates a sawing guide.)

mitre square a tool used to mark out or test angles of 45° on wood.

moisture content the amount of moisture in a piece of wood expressed as a percentage by weight. Timber for general purposes is seasoned to a moisture content of 20% but for most furniture a level of 12% is more appropriate.

mortise the slot which is cut to accept a tenon. (Ch.5)

mortise gauge the tool used to set out the dimensions of mortises and tenons when jointing.

mouldings lengths of wood which are machined to a particular section. Mouldings are used to improve appearance and to cover joins.

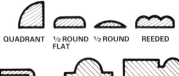

QUADRANT   ½ ROUND   ½ ROUND   REEDED
            FLAT

HOCKEY STICK   ASTRAGAL   EDGE BEAD

multiply a plywood which is made up of many thin veneers, and consequently is very strong and stable.

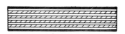

muntin a supporting member set into a frame to strengthen a panel.

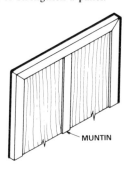

MUNTIN

N

nail punch (set) a punch which is used to drive a nail or pin head below the surface of the wood.

nominal size the width and thickness of sawn timber. Machine planed timber will be smaller than the nominal size by 3mm (about $\frac{1}{8}$in) or so in width and thickness and this must be allowed for. (Ch.1)

O

offcut waste pieces of timber produced when cutting to size.

oilstone a flat stone which is used to sharpen cutting tools, e.g. chisel and plane blades. The stone is soaked in oil to lubricate the sharpening process and to help float away the metal particles from the blades.

orbital sander a portable sanding machine which produces an orbital motion on a rubber pad, which is covered with an abrasive paper of an appropriate grade.

P

pad saw a small saw which can be used to cut fairly intricate shapes. Working from a drilled hole the saw can be used to work in the middle of a large area.

panel gauge a large gauge made of wood and used to mark out large dimensions on board materials.

panel saw a handsaw with cross-cut teeth suitable for cutting thin sheet materials such as plywood and hardboard.

particle board alternative name for chipboard.

pegboard hardboard drilled with a pattern of holes and used for display stands or where ventilation is required.

pein the end of a hammer head opposite to the striking face.

pencil gauge a simple gauging device made of a rebated block of wood which is used in conjunction with a pencil. Used where a cut line is not required, e.g. when marking out a chamfer.

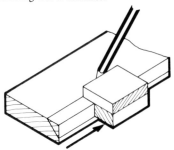

piling sticks the softwood sticks which are placed between the boards in a seasoning stack (fig.464).

pilot hole the hole drilled into a piece of wood to aid the insertion of a screw. (Ch.13)

pin hammer a small cross-pein hammer of a suitable weight to drive pins into wood.

pin push a tool which can be used to drive small pins into wood. It is particularly useful for driving pins into awkward places or as a means of positioning a pin to be driven in with a hammer.

pincers the tool used to extract nails or pins from wood, or to cut them to length.

plane iron the cutting blade of a plane (fig.471).

plank a term used to describe a piece of timber over 50mm (2in) thick.

plinth the platform on which a piece of furniture may be mounted. The platform may consist of a box or an open frame.

plough plane the plane used to cut grooves in wood. (Ch.10)

plug a piece of wood prepared to fill a hole either to make a repair or to cover a screwhead. A plug will often be made of a wood to match the workpiece.

plywood a manufactured board material which consists of thin wood veneers glued together with their grain directions alternated. A strong and stable material which is available in many different grades. (Ch.1)

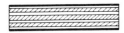

pocket an angled hole cut into the inside of a top rail of a table through which the table top can be screwed down. (Ch.13)

polyether foam a plastic foam material in very common use in furniture upholstery.

polyurethane the plastic material which is the basis of most modern paints and varnishes.

polyvinyl acetate (PVA) the material which forms the base of most woodworking adhesives suitable for internal furniture construction.

primer the first coat of paint to be applied to a job. Primer usually has a lead content and its purpose is to seal the surface and provide a stable base for the undercoat and gloss.

Q

quarter sawn quarter sawn timber produced by quarter or radial sawing is very stable and unlikely to warp (fig.478).

R

rail a horizontal member in a structure.

rasp a toothed tool like a coarse file used to remove material in shaped or sculptural work.

rebate a woodworking feature made by removing the edge of a panel or board. Rebates are usually cut to accept side or top panels.

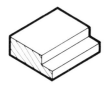

rebate plane plane used to cut rebates in timber. (Ch.10)

rip saw handsaw which has teeth which are designed to cut efficiently along the grain of timber.

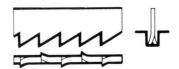

riving knife the knife which is mounted behind a circular saw blade to keep the sawcut in the wood open and prevent the wood closing onto the blade.

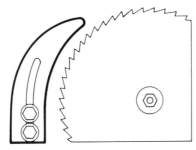

rosehead countersink the tool which is used in a drill to form the hollow into which a countersink head screw will lie flush. (Ch.13)

round head a type of screw which is mainly used to fix metal fittings to wood.

router a tool which can be set to depth and is used to cut below the surface of a piece of work. The router plane is a hand tool and is used to level the bottom of

ROUTER PLANE

POWER ROUTER

trenches or recessed areas. The power router is an extremely versatile machine which can also be used to cut out shapes in wood.

rubbed joint a method of jointing in which flat surfaces are glued and rubbed against one another to drive out the surplus glue in order to build up surface tension which will hold the joint in place.

S

sanding block a block of cork which is wrapped with abrasive paper for sanding. The block ensures an even pressure. (Ch.14)

sash cramp long workshop cramps used to hold workpieces together after glueing up. (Ch.15)

saw set the tool that is used to bend or set the teeth on a saw.

saw sharpener a tool which incorporates a triangular file and a guide which ensures that the saw teeth are filed, and therefore sharpened, at the correct angle.

scraper a tool which simply consists of a thin steel plate which can be used to finish a surface after planing or to obtain a finish on awkward grain. (Ch.14)

scratch stock a tool which can be easily made in the workshop. With the blade ground to the required shape the scratch stock will form mouldings along the grain.

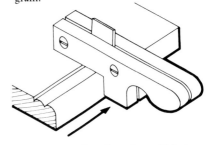

screw cup a shaped washer which increases the bearing area of a screw. This can be useful when a screw has to be withdrawn a number of times particularly with softwood. (Ch.13)

seasoning the process of drying timber out to make it stable and usable for furniture making or constructional work.

shake a defect in timber where the fibres have separated, usually along an annual ring. Shakes, which are only evident after felling, may mean the loss of much valuable timber.

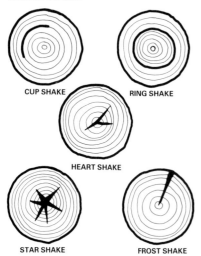

CUP SHAKE RING SHAKE

HEART SHAKE

STAR SHAKE FROST SHAKE

shank the stem or shaft of an object e.g. the plain part of a screw or drill.

shellac a material which is derived from insect secretion and which is used as a base for varnishes and finishing materials e.g. french polish.

shooting board a piece of workshop equipment which is used to prevent splitting when planing the ends of narrow pieces of wood square. (Ch.2)

short grain the weakness in wood is along the grain and short grain is a fault to be avoided, particularly when cutting shaped pieces from solid wood boards.

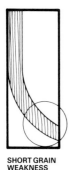

SHORT GRAIN WEAKNESS IMPROVED POSITIONING FOR STRENGTH

shoulder plane a plane with a low-angled blade which is mainly used to trim the shoulders of joints.

shrinkage plate a plate which is used to fix a solid wood table top onto its frame. The plate will allow the movement of the top which will take place in response to changes in humidity. (Ch.18)

side rebate plane a plane which can be used to widen or trim the sides of rebates or grooves.

silicon carbide a hard abrasive material which is used to make wet or dry paper.

sliding bevel a marking or testing tool which can be set to any desired angle.

slipstone a shaped sharpening oilstone which is mainly used for removing the burr when sharpening gouges.

smoothing plane a small bench plane which is used for small scale work and for finishing.

softwood a botanical term which identifies coniferous or needle-like leaved trees. As a rule the timber from these trees is physically soft.

spokeshave a type of plane which is used to smooth shaped work or to chamfer edges. The flat-soled spokeshave is used for flat or convex work and the curved-soled spokeshave for concave work.

stay a fitting which controls the movement of a door or lid. (Ch.18)

steam-bending some timbers become quite flexible when steamed in a steam chest and can be pulled into shapes which will set on cooling.

steel wool steel wool is useful for rubbing down between coats of varnish and also for applying wax when polishing.

stile the vertical members of a framework.

stock the main body of a tool, e.g. the wooden handles of squares.

stopper a filling material which is used to fill cracks, small gaps and to cover punched pin heads. Stopper is available in a range of colours to match common timbers.

stout heart plywood a plywood which consists of thin facing veneers either side of a thick veneer of a cheaper wood.

stretcher a rail which runs the length of a chair or table frame and ties the leg frames together.

surform tools a range of tools which has open-backed toothed blades. The tools

SURFORM FLAT FILE

SURFORM PLANE

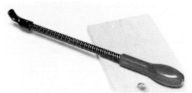

SURFORM ROUND FILE

SURFORM BLOCK PLANE

are particularly good for carving or sculptural work in wood or plaster.

T

tambour a sliding shutter consisting of narrow strips of wood glued to a material backing.

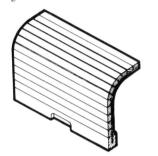

tape a flexible steel rule which is invaluable for measuring in the workshop.

teak oil an oil which makes a good preservative for timber out of doors.
template a shape prepared in card, hardboard or sheet metal to help with marking out or cutting.
tenon the projection which is fitted into the mortise in a mortise and tenon joint. (Ch.5)
tenon saw the back saw which is used for many sawing operations, including the sawing of tenons.

tongue and groove a weatherproof edge joint used in flooring and outbuilding construction. (Ch.9)

trimming knife a useful general purpose knife which can be used for marking out.

trying plane a long bench plane for working large areas or long edges.

try square a tool for marking out or testing angles of 90°.

turnbutton pivoting fixing device, often used to lock folding furniture flat.
turnscrew bit a bit which is fitted into a brace to drive large screws into place.

twist bits bits which are used to drill deep holes of quite small diameters.

twist drills general purpose drills for wood and metal. (Ch.16)

V

Velcro a touch-and-close fastening strip which can be useful for holding cushions in place and which has other upholstery applications.
veneer a thin sheet of wood which is used for surface decoration or in the construction of plywood.
vice a holding device which is essential for many bench operations.

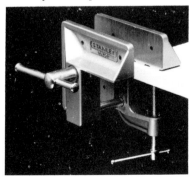

W

waney edge the edge of a board showing the natural edge of the tree, sometimes used to decorative effect.

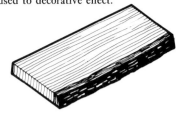

warping the curvature which may occur across the width of a board.
weatherboarding machined boards which are shaped in such a way that when they are overlapped horizontally they form a weatherproof joint. Used in the construction of outbuildings. (Ch.1)
webbing rubberised strips which are fitted to chair frames to give comfortable support to seating cushions. (Ch.19)
wedge tapered piece of wood used to tighten a joint by being driven into place. Folding wedges can provide a useful means of exerting pressure on an assembly.

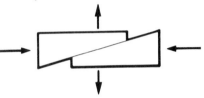

winding strips parallel-sided hardwood strips which are used to test visually the flatness of a board, frame or surface.

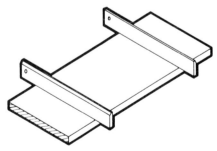

wobble saw a circular saw blade which is mounted between angled washers and set to cut grooves of the required width and depth.

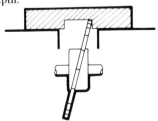

Conversion table

For greater accuracy work to $\frac{1}{32}$in. This is calculated by dividing the measurement in millimetres by 25.4; the figures following the decimal point are then converted to the nearest fraction by reading off from the table below.

Decimal fraction	Unit fraction	Decimal fraction	Unit fraction
0.03125	$\frac{1}{32}$	**0.625**	$\frac{5}{8}$
0.0625	$\frac{1}{16}$	0.65625	$\frac{21}{32}$
0.09375	$\frac{3}{32}$	0.6875	$\frac{11}{16}$
0.125	$\frac{1}{8}$	0.71875	$\frac{23}{32}$
0.15625	$\frac{5}{32}$	**0.75**	$\frac{3}{4}$
0.1875	$\frac{3}{16}$	0.78125	$\frac{25}{32}$
0.21875	$\frac{7}{32}$	0.8125	$\frac{13}{16}$
0.25	$\frac{1}{4}$	0.84375	$\frac{27}{32}$
0.28125	$\frac{9}{32}$	**0.875**	$\frac{7}{8}$
0.3125	$\frac{5}{16}$	0.90625	$\frac{29}{32}$
0.34375	$\frac{11}{32}$	0.9375	$\frac{15}{16}$
0.375	$\frac{3}{8}$	0.96875	$\frac{31}{32}$
0.40625	$\frac{13}{32}$		
0.4375	$\frac{7}{16}$		
0.46875	$\frac{15}{32}$		
0.5	$\frac{1}{2}$		
0.53125	$\frac{17}{32}$		
0.5625	$\frac{9}{16}$		
0.59375	$\frac{19}{32}$		

e.g to convert 320mm to imperial measurements, divide by 25.4; this equals 12.598425in ($0.59375 = \frac{19}{32}$) = $12\frac{19}{32}$in.

Manufacturers and suppliers

U.K.

Aaronson Bros. Ltd
Conti Products Division
Aro House
18/19 Long Lane
London E.C.2
  Melamine-faced and veneered chipboard (Contiplas &
  Contiboard) edging strip and corner joints

Bahco Record Tools Ltd
Parkway Works
Sheffield
  Most woodworking hand tools under the brand names
  of Record, Marples, Ridgway and Tyzack

Black and Decker Ltd
Cannon Lane
Maidenhead
Berkshire
  A wide range of portable power tools, woodworking
  machinery and workshop equipment

Borden U.K. Ltd
Humbrol
Hull
  Stoppers and Cascamite adhesive, also Humbrol enamel
  paints

Ciba Geigy Plastics & Additives Co.
Duxford
Cambridge
  Araldite, Aerodux, Aerolite and Aerocol PVA adhesives

Clam-Brummer Ltd
Maxwell Road
Borehamwood
Hertfordshire
  Stoppers, fillers and adhesives

Cornerjoints Ltd
Unit 7
Batford Mill Trading Estate
Lower Luton Road
Harpenden
Hertfordshire
  Corner jointing systems, catches, hinges, stays, edging
  strips and other fittings and accessories

Dunlop Ltd
Chester Road,
Erdington
Birmingham
  A range of adhesives including Thixofix contact
  adhesive

Dunlopillo Division U.K.
Hirwaun Industrial Estate
Aberdare
Glamorgan
  Latex and polyether upholstery foams

Evode Ltd
Common Road
Stafford
  A wide range of adhesives including Resin W and
  impact glue, also Furniglas PU15 varnishes

Fitchett and Woollacott Ltd
Willow Road
Lenton Lane
Nottingham
  Stockists of a wide range of softwoods, hardwoods and
  manufactured board materials

International Paint
24–30 Canute Road
Southampton
Hampshire
  Woodplan varnishes and preservatives, paints and
  enamels for wood and metal

Isaac Lord Ltd
Desborough Road
High Wycombe
Buckinghamshire
  Stockists of a wide range of cabinet fittings and
  hardware items, also some tools and workshop
  equipment. Mail order service

Neill Tools Ltd
Napier Street
Sheffield
  Woodworking tools under the brand name of Eclipse

Pirelli Ltd
Derby Road
Burton-on-Trent
Staffordshire
  Webbing and seating platforms

Plasplugs Ltd
Sheridon House
Vernon Street
Derby
  Cabinet fittings, jointing systems, small tools and fixing
  plugs

Sadolin (UK) Ltd
Tower Close
St Peter's Industrial Park
Huntingdon
Cambridgeshire
  A wide range of clear and coloured varnishes and wood
  preservatives

Stanley Tools Ltd
Woodside
Sheffield
  A wide range of woodworking handtools and workshop
  equipment

Sterling Roncraft Ltd
Chapeltown
Sheffield
  Finishing materials including Colron wood dyes and
  Translac varnishes

Trent Valley Plastics
Anglesey Road
Burton-on-Trent
Staffordshire
  Plastic mouldings and edging strips and the Sheerglide
  plastic drawer system

Woodfit Ltd
Kem Mill
Chorley
Lancashire
  A mail order service for a very wide range of cabinet
  fittings and hardware items

Woodmen
104 Churchill Road
Bicester
Oxfordshire
  Stockists of a range of makes of woodworking
  machinery. Showroom and mail order service

U.S.A.
Southern Lumber Co.
1402 S. First St
San Jose 95110
California

Tech Plywood & Lumber Co.
110 Webb St
Hamden 06511
Connecticut

Paul Bunyan Hardwood Centre
12658 Paulina St
Calumet Park 60643
Illinois

Amherst Wood Working
Hubbard Ave
Northampton 01060
Massachusetts

Quality Woods
Box 205
Lake Hiawatha 07034
New Jersey

Index